Tragic Thought
and the
Grammar
of Tragic Myth

Tragic Thought and the Grammar of Tragic Myth

BRADLEY BERKE

Indiana University Press
Bloomington

Manufactured in the United States of America

Library of Congress Cataloging in Publication Data

Berke, Bradley, 1949-
  Tragic thought and the grammar of tragic myth.

  Bibliography: p.
  1. Tragedy.   2. Tragic, The.   I. Title
PN1892.B42   808.2'512'0141   81-48675
                                            AACR2
1   2   3   4   5   86   85   84   83   82

ISBN 0-253-36027-7

Contents

Introduction   1

1. **Tragic Thought**

1,i.   The Tragic   5

1,ii. Tragic Thought: Ethical and Aesthetic   5

1,iii. Tragic Myth   10

1,iv. Tragic Pleasure, Its Intensity, and Its Dosage   14

2. **Belief and Information**

2,i.   Belief as a Result of Understanding Information   16

2,ii. The Presentation of Information in Works of Art   18

2,iii. Mimesis and Symbolism   22

2,iv. Conclusion   24

3. **A Grammar of Tragic Myth**

3,i.   The Writer-Spectator's Intuition and the Understanding
       of Tragic Myth   25

3,ii. The Scope of the Grammar of Tragic Myth   26

3,iii. The Form of the Grammar of Tragic Myth   28

3,iv. Conventions for Applying the Rules of the Grammar   30

3,v.   The Rules of the Grammar of Tragic Myth   32

3,vi. Tragic Plots, Coplots, and Subplots   66

3,vii. Generation versus Scansion   73

4. **The Central Desire Triangle of Tragic Myth**

    4,i.   Landmarks   75

    4,ii. *Troilus and Cressida*   77

5. **Tragic and Nontragic Variants**

    5,i.   Differences in Plot and Differences in Purpose   82

    5,ii. Euripides' *Hippolytus*   83

    5,iii. *Phèdre*   84

    5,iv. The Portrayal of Character Traits and their
            Practical Value   86

    5,v. Situations versus Plots   88

Conclusion   90

Appendix: The Morphology of Information in Art

    A,i.   Critical Categories   94

    A,ii. The Standardization of Informational Contents   94

    A,iii. Subjects and Predicates   95

    A,iv. Predicate Types   99

    A,v. Noun Phrases and Nouns   103

Notes   110

Bibliography   115

Tragic Thought
and the
Grammar
of Tragic Myth

Introduction

The following study attempts to establish the bases for an integrated theory of the tragic genre. This theory consists of a formal description of the conceptual system underlying the creation and appreciation of individual, existing tragedies and a somewhat less formal and ultimately speculative explanation of the aesthetic effectiveness of tragic works. Above all, the theory must be descriptively adequate. Descriptive adequacy involves formally characterizing all and only those phenomena that appear to be genuine manifestations of the conceptual system under consideration. In the case of tragedy, these phenomena include not only actualized examples of the genre but also eventually actualizable ones. Thus, a descriptive account of the tragic system must surpass any tangible corpus, in order to predict the full range of possibilities inherent in the system. It is also important that our theory be general. That is, it should analyze and identify the elements of the tragic system in terms of hypothetical constructs independently established by general theories, such as theories of formal logic and linguistics. The hypothetical constructs in question should represent both substantive and formal universals, i.e., ultimately transcendental concepts and patterns of combining them. For example, if, in discussing tragedies, we should use terms like "subject," "significant element," and "plot," we should like our usage to correspond to the usage of the most adequate theories of logic, semiotics, and criticism, as the case may be. By rendering our theory as general as possible, we hope to facilitate associations with other points of view.

From these associations may arise new insights and a sharpening of traditional conceptualizations.

Although its primary goals are descriptive adequacy and maximal generality, our theory should be both practicable and adaptable. Although they do not affect its validity in any way, these qualities may determine the acceptance or rejection of a descriptively adequate theory. That is, they are useful in choosing the best theory from among a potentially great number of theories of equal descriptive adequacy. By practicability, we mean manageability; a practicable theory will be relatively simple and elegant. Thus, to the extent that didactic considerations permit, we shall strive for an economy of terms, symbols, rules, etc. Adaptability is somewhat more difficult to define than practicability. Briefly, a theory is adaptable when it is written in a form applicable to other theories concerned with related systems. For example, it will become clear in further discussions that our theory of the tragic genre is at least partially based on a formal description of the structure of tragic plots. Thus, since the theory presented here is an account of tragedy as a specifically literary and, even more particularly, dramatic genre, its adaptability can be determined on the basis of the applicability of its descriptions of plot structure to the plot structures of nondramatic and even nonliterary tragic works. In summary, we want our theory to be descriptively adequate, simple, and elegant for the sake of dealing critically with tragedy, and we want it to be general and adaptable for the sake of measuring it against other theories of tragedy and objects related to tragedy.

The tragic system, like any other system, is an arrangement of interrelated hypothetical constructs. While describing this arrangement, an "integrated" theory of the tragic genre will attempt to explain the aesthetic effectiveness of actual manifestations of the tragic system. That is, it will explain the role of tragic works in the process of artistic pleasure-production. A number of speculative hypotheses will constitute our explanatory remarks. Although they may be neither proven nor provable, these hypotheses can be justified on the basis of their contribution to the predictive power of the descriptive component of our theory. It must be noted that nothing in this descriptive component "follows" from our explanatory hypotheses and that nothing in our explanatory hypotheses "follows" from this descriptive component. On the contrary, our explanatory remarks are meant solely to provide some presentive significance to the purely formal descriptive aspects of our theory. If insights associated with our explanatory hypotheses seem to indicate descriptive choices, they are, nonetheless, far from constituting discovery procedures. Thus, our approach is hypothetical but neither deductive nor inductive; its genesis involves "reasonable" speculation and not logical necessity.

We maintain that tragedies are perceptible objects and that their principal aesthetic "usefulness" lies in their common informational contents. The essential information expressed in all tragedies serves in producing a state of belief, and this state of belief is accompanied by the experience of feelings of intense pleasure. Because it is not self-evident that any particular bit of information is expressed in all tragedies, we shall have to demonstrate and to explain how apparently nonsynonymous forms of expression can be semiotically associated with a unique (semantic) content.

Our demonstration will be formal and descriptive; our explanation will be hypothetical. We shall posit the existence of an innate human faculty for understanding intelligible expressions of information. As a part of this "semiotic intuition," we shall posit a specific faculty for understanding artistic expressions of information, and, as a part of this specific faculty, an even more specific faculty for understanding expressions of the information essential to the production of tragic pleasure, which we shall call the "writer-spectator's intuition concerning tragedy." The formal description of the "writer-spectator's intuition" involves the establishment of a "psychological performance model," a set of rules describing "universal," i.e., "regular" acts of expression and understanding. We shall present a "tragic grammar" based on a hypothetical psychological performance model for the expression and understanding of the essential information contained in tragedies.

Because of the introductory nature of this work, we shall concentrate more heavily on presenting a conceptual framework for the study of tragedy than on illustrating the possible applications of a method. Thus, any conclusions or perspectives we might propose on the basis of our descriptive formalizations will only be by way of example. In discussing various aspects of tragedy, we shall attempt to show how the conceptual framework to be presented here is particularly well adapted to their investigation. However, at this stage, it would be impossible to list all of the advantages (and disadvantages) of our approach. Finally, although a detailed exploration of the artistic, psychological, and philosophical implications of this conceptual framework would, undoubtedly, be useful in situating it in an intellectual tradition, we shall be content to let the predictive power of the descriptive component of our theory stand as a self-explanatory proof of the theoretical gains achieved here over other theories of the tragic genre.

Chapter One

Tragic Thought

1,i. The Tragic

In the following discussion, we shall attempt to characterize "tragic thought," as we imagine it. By "tragic thought," we mean a particular philosophical mode, specifically an ideology. We take tragic thought to be ubiquitous in and typical of Western culture. Thus, although it has certainly appeared in other civilizations, we shall be primarily concerned with its manifestations in the West. In this context, we wish to emphasize that tragic thought has not depended on tragedy, i.e., on a certain form of dramatic art, for its expression. On the contrary, from the outset, it has flourished in philosophy and religion as well as in art. Some of the most valuable insights into the essence of the tragic, as we recognize it, have come to us precisely from philosophical and religious sources ranging from Anaximander to Camus and from Genesis to Calvin and Pascal. Of course, art, philosophy, and religion have often shared common purposes, especially aesthetic ones, and it should prove interesting to compare artistic and nonartistic expressions of tragic thought. We shall begin our discussion of this philosophical mode with some schematic metaphilosophical considerations, in order strategically to situate it among other related modes of thought.

1,ii. Tragic Thought: Ethical and Aesthetic

All "ethical" modes of thought address themselves to the fundamental question:
1) Does existence have a meaning?

(We need not be concerned here with the vagueness of this question or with the enormity of its implications. The term "meaning" may be interpreted loosely to mean anything from "value" to "interest" to "significance.") Whether they resolve this question affirmatively or negatively, "ethical" modes do not necessarily inquire into the nature of the meaning of existence. On the contrary, only what we might call "aesthetic ethical" modes attempt to deal with the further question:

2) What is the meaning of existence?

(We may say the same of this question as we have said of the previous one.) Tragic thought is an "aesthetic ethical" mode of thought in that it deals with question 2. It distinguishes itself from other "aesthetic ethical" modes on the basis of the answer it gives to question 2. These points may be illustrated by comparing tragic thought to three other "ethical" modes: positivism, nihilism, and existentialism.

If we designate those "ethical" modes that attribute a meaning to existence as "affirmative" modes and those that do not as "negative," we can establish the following schema:

	Affirmative	Negative
Aesthetic	Tragic Thought	Existentialism
Nonaesthetic	Positivism	Nihilism

Neither the nihilist nor the positivist is concerned with determining the nature of the meaning of existence. The nihilist, certain that existence has no meaning, rejects any attempt to discover a meaning in it as an absurdity. His positivist counterpart, satisfied with the present order, recognizes a meaning in that order, a meaning whose appreciation seems to him so simple that he need not reflect on it. By comparison, the tragic thinker and the existentialist, initially unsure whether or not existence has a meaning, attempt to decide the question by first exploring just what such a meaning might be. Asking what the nature of the meaning of existence might be suggests a desire to know, a desire which betrays a lack of assurance. The anxiety accompanying this lack of assurance has, at repeated moments in history, been a sign of psychological conflict among the members of society in the face of what have been perceived by cultural historians, with or without justification, as unusually extreme contrasts in social conditions.[1] In any case, it is this anxiety that gives rise to the need for an aesthetic solution to the problem of existence. Positivist thought is not aesthetically motivated because it is not anxious thought. On the other hand, the anxiety that causes doubt about the meaning of existence must not be a source of despair, for despair, like complacency, excludes the possibility of aesthetic solutions. Therefore, nihilism, i.e., desperate thought, like positivism, is basically nonaesthetic. Finally, tragic thought and at least one form of existentialism—that expressed by Camus in *Le Mythe de Sisyphe,* for example—are aesthetic ethical modes, because they are motivated by an anxiety without despair. As we have indicated, tragic thought is an affirmative ethical mode, whereas existentialism is a negative one. The aesthetic superiority of tragic thought over existentialism, as evidenced by the former's relative predominance in Western culture, undoubtedly stems from this fact.

Existentialist thought maintains that existence has no predetermined meaning. It does not, however, begin with the assumption that existence has no meaning at all. In fact, some forms of existentialism seek, aesthetically, to render existence tolerable by assigning a (possible) meaning to existence, that justifies, in a practical sense, life's pains. It is clear, of course, that existentialist thought never attempts to discern the meaning of existence by opposing existence to that which is not existence. On the contrary, it tries to determine this meaning by contrasting different "modes of being." Thus, in a nonlogical way, it succeeds in determining what, logically, amounts to the meaning(s) of these modes and not that of existence itself. In other words, to oppose "being" (*l'être*) to "nothingness" (*le néant*) is to beg the question of the meaning of existence. As we have said, existentialist thought does ask itself this question. Nevertheless, it is generally the case that existentialist thinkers, in their preoccupation with "being," have dealt too lightly with the problem of existence. As a result, existentialist aesthetics is less concerned with establishing the conviction that existence, with its inherent suffering, is tolerable than with developing the notion that there are tolerable modes of being. In other words, the significant act that constitutes a mode of being is seen also as providing some motivation for existing. It is necessary to posit some sort of contentment immanent in the individual's commitment to a significant act: "Il faut imaginer Sisyphe heureux." That this contentment is sufficient to justify existing is doubtful. In any case, by refusing to oppose existence to that which is not existence, existentialism implicitly admits that existence has no meaning at all. In the final analysis, there emerges the absurd combination of significant being and meaningless existence.

Tragic thought does not rely on absurdity. By directly attacking the problem of existence, tragic thought does not deny the profound and immediate feeling of unhappiness that first causes man's doubt about the meaning of existence. Unhappiness, like happiness, is an integral part of existence, and the tragic thinker's conscious or unconscious purpose is to render existence tolerable by making it more happy than unhappy. Whatever happiness man experiences in life, existence must seem to him relatively unhappy. This unhappiness derives from his naive belief that the desiring and suffering of existence will never cease, that even death will not necessarily end them. The tragic thinker must dispel this belief, and he does so by claiming that there is a state that is not existence, viz., nonexistence, from which desiring and suffering are absent and to which one can eventually accede. It will become clear that, although the tragic thinker feels that man can be relatively happy (in life) by believing that he will eventually accede to nonexistence, the tragic thinker apparently does not want access to nonexistence to be taken for granted.

If the individual imagined that death led unconditionally to nonexistence, he would, undoubtedly, seek immediate death through suicide. Because the tragic thinker's aesthetic purpose is doubled by a prosocial one, he must claim that nonexistence is not the only state occurring after death. The pro-social purpose of the tragic thinker is simply to keep the individual more or less willingly alive and useful to society. This purpose is particularly difficult to accomplish since the individual probably sees the social order, with its apparently endless desire-gratification cycle, as the source of suffering. More precisely, he sees, in the "actants" (formal participants in his intentionally created social universe) the "concrete" perpetuators of the desire-gratification cycle from which he wishes to escape. Although tragic thinkers have had theoretically to prevent the individual from destroying these "enemies," in reality, they have accepted the impossibility of convincing him that he can attain nonexistence without at least vicariously destroying them.

The tragic thinker "stages" the destruction of the social order in the imaginary realm of myth. We shall call this destruction of the social order by the individual "self-annihilation," for reasons that can be clearly illustrated in a formal description of tragic myth.[2] In tragic myth, the act of self-annihilation involves an agent and a patient both of whom represent one and the same mythical self-annihilator. The agent function is fulfilled by an "actant" that we shall call the "Accomplishing Subject" or "Hero." The patient function is fulfilled by the formal participants in the social order as it is intentionally conceived, i.e., by "actants" that we shall call the "Desirer," the "Desired Object," and the "Legal Authority" (the guardian principle that makes the Desired Object more or less obtainable). Whereas the "Hero" represents the active, antisocial aspect of the mythical self-annihilator, the other actants represent, jointly, the passive social aspects of this imaginary figure.

Staging the destruction of the social order enables the tragic thinker to accomplish two purposes. First, he can "show" that this destruction is possible. Second, he can "stipulate" under what conditions it is possible. What is important here is that the tragic thinker makes these conditions seem difficult to attain, but not impossible. He claims that the individual who is in a position to achieve nonexistence must possess the same qualities as both the "Hero" and the "Desirer." That is, he must be both awesome and miserable, a great doer and a great sufferer. Because conceiving of oneself as possessing these qualities constitutes both flattery to the ego and fuel for self-pity, the individual in the tragic thinker's audience might identify himself readily enough with the mythical self-annihilator. Nevertheless, he cannot delude himself entirely and must be able to support this identification with certain "concrete" proofs. In this way, the tragic thinker can impel the individual actually to suffer for society and to aim for observable (socially desirable) greatness, in order to qualify as one deserving of nonexistence. Finally, through an aesthetic identification with an imaginary figure, the individual can "liquidate" his desire to destroy the social order without really destroying society. That is, he can "repress" this desire, as if he were "postponing" its gratification. This postponement of gratification and the continuation of the "tension" (*Unlust*) associated with the maintenance of a state of desire is made possible by the gratification of the greater desire for assurance that the sufferings of existence are worthwhile.

1,iii. Tragic Myth

In staging the imaginary destruction of the social order, the tragic thinker portrays "criminal" acts. It can be assumed that the individual has no great natural love for society; thus, to assert that these acts are socially undesirable is not a basis sufficient for convincing the individual that they are criminal. For this reason, the tragic thinker must appeal to some "Cosmic" or superhuman authority. He claims that the destruction of the social order is a crime against the Cosmos. However, intuiting the individual's basic hatred for society, he does not "over-defend" it by claiming that the destruction of the social order is the greatest crime against the Cosmos or that the Cosmos is particularly fond of the social order. On the contrary, the tragic thinker claims, if only implicitly, that what is most dear to the

Cosmos is chaos and that man, with his "ordering" intentionality, offends the Cosmos most grievously by his very existence. Nietzsche, in his attempt to characterize tragic thought, notes that tragic culture in the West begins with the assumption that suffering is a proof of the injustice of life. That is, suffering, as a form of expiation, suggests that all those who suffer, i.e. all those who exist, are, in some sense, criminal. Finally, the destruction of the social order is a crime against the Cosmos, because it brings with it an end to the expiation of the crime of existence. If one, by his very existence, commits a crime against the Cosmos, then he doubly offends that Cosmos by attempting to escape his punishment, i.e., by seeking nonexistence. If the Cosmos "allows" certain (mythical) figures to escape from the expiation of the crime of existence, it is because it esteems that they have suffered greatly and that their peculiar greatnesses entitle them to pardon and reward.

Tragic thinkers in the West have developed two basic mythical versions of this ethical model. These versions derive primarily from two separate cultural influences: the Greek and the Judaeo-Christian. For the Greeks and for classical tragedy, in general, the basic cultural datum is the criminality of life. Classical tragedy, in stressing the criminality of life, chooses to concentrate on its ethical counterpart, the criminality of escape from life. Thus, it focuses attention on the criminal act(s) whose commission leads to nonexistence; that is, it focuses on the destruction of the social order. The depressing aspect of life is neglected in favor of the exaltation of eternal peace. Pity and fear, the unpleasant emotions of life, are forgotten in the face of the true emotions of classical tragedy, namely, Boileau's "douce terreur" and "pitié charmante" or what A. C. Bradley calls "awe." Aristotle takes the end for the means: as a Greek, he is culturally preoccupied with suffering, pity, and fear, and assumes that tragedy deals directly with these phenomena. In fact, it deals with them, aesthetically, by glorifying their opposites.

One might argue that classical tragedy confirms Aristotelian doctrine only in its preoccupation with the superior individual. It depicts only certain men, the "supermen," who deserve, in the most positive sense, the annihilation they seek. Although the "tragic hero," like any other mortal, is guilty of the crime of existence, he is never held responsible for his act of self-deliverance. On the contrary, the responsibility for this "crime" is always attributed to Fate or to the gods, who take hold of certain individuals and alienate them from themselves. Hamlet, for example, perceives the difference between the hero and the ordinary man. He sees that it is perfectly possible to "suffer the slings and arrows of outrageous fortune" and knows, without really asking, that it is "nobler in the mind," i.e., heroic but abnormal "to take arms against a sea of troubles and by opposing end them." Since the hero does not choose to act for his own deliverance, it must be that his personal qualities cause the gods to choose for him. In this way, it is demonstrated that the ordinary man need not commit any criminal act; rather, he need only possess those (socially desirable) qualities that might cause the gods to favor him. Finally, it might be added that mimetic art[3] is particularly well suited to fostering the kind of identification required in classical tragedy; for, logically and psychologically, one relates best to an imaginary agent through his acts.

In many ways, the Bible resembles works of mimetic art. Like classical tragedy, it portrays a heroic act: Adam's fall. However, this act, and not the basic criminality of life, is the basic cultural datum of Judaeo-Christian tradition. "Original" sin is really the second crime in the tragic series, i.e. the crime of escaping from (earthly) existence. Eden (*le Paradis terrestre*) is as dull and devoid of hope as the world before Prometheus' fire and Pandora's box. Here, no aesthetic identification is necessary between the ordinary individual and the tragic hero. The tradition simply stipulates: "In Adam's fall, we sinned all." Thus, every man is guaranteed the hero's privilege and the possibility of salvation, but there is still a condition to the attainment of Paradise. As in classical tragedy, the Judaeo-Christian model insists on the ethical counterpart of that which is to be stressed, viz. the heroic act of "original sin." The criminality of Adam's fall lies in its being an escape from the punishment of the primordial crime of existence. Again, life in Eden before the fall is not really happy. The Judaeo-Christian tragic thinker focuses on the crime of existence, or, rather, on the suffering that marks its expiation. If the ordinary man is to benefit from Adam's act, he must be a sufferer, and it is with the sufferer, the captive, and the slave (in the Nietzschean sense) that an aesthetic identification must take place. Christianity has even gone so far as to create a suffering and crucified God, as an "antihero," in order to concentrate this identification.[4] Finally, unlike the authors of classical tragedies, Judaeo-Christian thinkers have accepted what Aristotle says about the effectiveness of pity and fear as tragic emotions, yet they still reject the notion of undeserved misfortune and repudiate the concept of the superior individual.

The recapitulate, the tragic thinker, through mimesis, brings about an aesthetic identification of the individual with the mythical self-annihilator in order to circumvent the individual's basic desire to escape from (social) existence. In so doing, he helps to fulfill another of the individual's wishes, the wish for assurance, assurance that, with perseverance and (socially useful) work, man can attain nonexistence, a sort of life without suffering and desire. In the following chapters, we shall attempt to demonstrate how the tragic Ur-myth of self-annihilation can be presented in many forms, how the imitation of this general activity can be enacted in imitations of complexes of specific actions. We shall concentrate mainly on dramatic presentations of the tragic myth, i.e., on the literary and specifically theatrical genre known as "tragedy," first, because dramatic tragedies, as opposed to nondramatic ones, form a traditionally constituted unit and, second, because religious, as opposed to artistic, presentations of tragic myth are too unvaried to be of interest in demonstrating how different stories can systematically be generated from one Ur-myth, while maintaining its informational content intact.

1,iv. Tragic Pleasure, Its Intensity, and Its Dosage

Tragic myth has always been related to ritual. In the face of life's difficulties, large and small, the individual constantly needs reassurance and re-demonstration of the mythical archetypes to which he must conform, in order to attain nonexistence. Thus, theatergoing for the ancient Greeks was as much a religious praxis as churchgoing for the Christian believer. It is at least partially for this reason that mankind has sought the key to the tragic in the production of a state of belief. Belief depends on evidence, and, each time everyday experience "proves" that there is no reason to believe that suffering and desire will ever cease, the individual needs to be "shown," through an expression of tragic myth, that there is every reason to believe that suffering and desire can cease.

It is the extreme intensity of the pleasure associated with tragic belief that has led us to our conception of the nature of that belief. The toleration of suffering, rather than being a mark of unhappy resignation, is an indication of general contentment, and it is difficult to overstate the extent to which physical suffering alone is tolerated by those who believe that, by suffering, they will attain "eternal peace." Finding subjective testimony concerning the intensity of tragic pleasure is relatively easy. A most concise and convincing theoretical identification of the feelings evoked by tragic myth, for example, is expressed in the following passage by A. C. Bradley:

> More important are other impressions. Sometimes from the very furnace of affliction a conviction seems borne to us that somehow, if we could only see it, this agony counts as nothing against the heroism and love which appear in it and thrill our hearts. Sometimes we are driven to cry out that these mighty or heavenly spirits who perish are too great for the little space in which they move, and that they vanish not into nothingness but into freedom. Sometimes from these sources and from others comes a presentiment, formless but haunting and even profound, that all the fury of conflict, with its waste and woe, is less than half the truth, "such stuff as dreams are made on."[5]

We take the generic, or genre-defining, uniqueness of the thrill, the exaltation in heroism and love, the belief in a "Nirvana-like" freedom, and the relative indifference to waste and woe as axiomatic. Our chief objective, in this work, will be to discover the element or elements common to all tragedies that evoke these feelings and, consequently, to show how the presence of such an element or elements in a work can serve as a primary criterion for characterizing that work as a tragic one.

Chapter Two

Belief and Information

2,i. Belief as a Result of Understanding Information

We wish, then, to identify at least one of the sources of the pleasurable feelings evoked by tragedy. These feelings are associated with a state of belief, and their source lies in the source of tragic belief. Believing involves understanding and reacting to perceived patterns of semiotically significant elements. The source of tragic belief lies in the presentation of certain information, which we have called tragic myth. Since it is not self-evident that the information constituting tragic myth, as we have described it, is presented in all tragedies, we shall have to show how it is expressed in them in different ways. In order to do so, we propose certain working hypotheses concerning the nature of the process of understanding information, in general, and, more particularly, concerning the nature of the process of understanding information contained in works of art.

To begin, we take the general process of understanding to involve the *performance* of certain acts. These acts constitute psychologically determined reactions to the perception of significant utterances. We imagine the psychological determination of these reactions to be partially innate and partially learned. On the one hand, we posit that the individual possesses an innate capacity or faculty for expressing and understanding information according to "regular," universal patterns; and, on the other hand, we posit that the individual exhibits this capacity through his manipulation of a specific, learned semiotic code.

The individual's innate capacity for expressing and understanding information, as it is exhibited through manipulation of specific semiotic codes, can be accounted for by a set of "rules" describing "regular" acts. We shall call this set of rules a "psychological performance model" for the expression and understanding of information. We shall call the innate capacity described by a psychological performance model for the expression and understanding of information the individual's "semiotic intuition."

The individual perceives an intelligible utterance and reacts to it in a specific way. When this reaction to the perception of an intelligible utterance is "normal" or "appropriate," we can call it a belief-reaction.[1] A "normal" or "appropriate" reaction to the perception of an intelligible utterance is one that is most often associated with the understanding of some specific informational content, one that indicates that the semiotic code being used "works" as a means of communication. We shall assume, for the purposes of this discussion, that the most direct way in which any given informational content may be expressed is in the form of simple declarative sentences corresponding to the so-called kernel sentences of (early) transformational generative grammar.[2] Of course, the information expressed in "kernel-type" sentences can also be expressed in other grammatical sentences, as well as in nongrammatical utterances. However, in understanding non-kernel-type sentences or nongrammatical but intelligible utterances, the individual must recapitulate, in reverse, the generative process by which these utterances are produced from kernel-type sentences. On arriving at a kernel-type sentence, the individual must also recapitulate, in reverse, the generative process through which that sentence is produced from manifestations of universal logical categories. When and only when the complete derivational[3] history of an intelligible utterance is established, can the individual react to it in a specific way. In the case of tragedy, the specific belief-reaction in which we are interested consists of pleasurable feelings and their behavioral, i.e., sociological, consequences.

2,ii. The Presentation of Information in Works of Art

As we have explained, in the case of the artistic tragic thinker, the artist must portray the accomplishment of desires. The ways in which the artist can portray the accomplishment of any given desire are multiple, and, since this multiplicity of possibilities for expression is peculiar to the artist's situation, it deserves our attention here. One of the things the artist cannot do is forthrightly to indicate to the desiring beholder of the work of art that he is portraying the accomplishment of one or more of that beholder's everyday desires. Precisely because they are everyday desires, the individual has learned to bear the experiences of feelings of pain that go along with them more or less well and not to think too much about them. Of course, he will bear them even better once the artist renders them completely "unconscious," i.e., represses them, but, since the artist must "play on them," the beholder must first suffer the increase of pain involved in being reminded of them. If this increase is too great, the beholder will avoid the artist's work. Thus, the artist must play on the individual's desires without throwing them in his face. In Aristotelian terms, the process of evoking and subsequently re-repressing ungratifiable desires might be called "cathartic." In psychoanalytic terms, a process like the one we have described is said to involve the emergence of disguised unconscious desires through a conscious censorship and their subsequent gratification. Whatever one might wish to call the process in question, it constrains the artist in a very particular way. Although he must make certain that the message remains intelligible, the artist must present the information that some given desire is accomplished in an "obscured" form. That is to say, the beholder of a work of art should be "forewarned" that even if the significant elements the artist uses to express himself are arranged in a "grammatical" way according to some semiotic system in whose use both the artist and the beholder are competent, he is never to take the superficial "meaning" (or "unmeaning") of these arrangements as the essential semantic content of the information the artist wishes to convey. This "convention," according to which the artist and the beholder communicate, distinguishes the presentation of works of art from that of such things as journalistic or didactic works.

There are two basic ways of transforming "kernel-sentence-type" arrangements of significant elements into intelligible but "non-kernel-sentence-type" arrangements, with respect to a given semantic content, and the artist uses both of them. First, one can replace "meaningful," "kernel-sentence-type" arrangements with manifestly "meaningless," i.e., ungrammatical, arrangements of significant elements; and, second, one can replace "meaningful" "kernel-sentence-type" arrangements with other meaningful arrangements, but conventionally discount the apparent "meaningfulness" of these arrangements. Naturally, in both cases, the resulting arrangements must be "derivable" from the initial ones by the application of the rules of what we have called a psychological performance model (for the understanding of the informational contents of works of art). Before discussing the nature of such a model, we might illustrate some typical replacement situations.

It must be noted that replacements of grammatical arrangements of significant elements by ungrammatical arrangements are never directly involved in obscuring information concerning the accomplishment of desires. On the other hand, they are instrumental in "complicating" the process of understanding works as wholes. That is, they increase the number of steps required to render intelligible expressions totally meaningful. The "unscrambling" of these replacements can constitute a pleasurable, playlike activity in itself, and psychoanalysis has recognized the strategic value of such activities in "seducing" the beholder of the work of art to relax his inhibitions in spite of the evocation of his desires.[4] In any case, the replacements in question here constitute part of what we might call "poetic license" or figurative usage in works of art. Cases of metonymy and allegorical personification provide simple examples. Instead of saying: "I saw three ships floating in the bay," one might say:

"I saw three sails floating in the bay." Of course, sails do not float, and, even if they did, we would not be interested in them. We know, through habit and convention, that something else is meant, and that something else is "ships." Instead of saying: "A pompous old man was blowing smoke rings," one might say: "A caterpillar was blowing smoke rings." Naturally, caterpillars do not blow smoke rings, but we know how to understand the proposition. Frequently, replacing grammatical arrangements with other grammatical arrangements serves the same purpose as replacing them with ungrammatical ones. Metaphors of all sorts provide examples here. When the poet says that Apollo has driven his chariot across the sky three times, we are given to understand that three days have passed. When he speaks of the "grim reaper," we know he is speaking of death. Finally, these replacements help in making it apparent to the individual that he is dealing with a work of art and that the intelligible expressions he recognizes in it are not to be taken "literally."

We have yet to discuss the most interesting group of replacement situations. These situations all involve the replacement of grammatical arrangements by other grammatical arrangements with a view to obscuring the evocation of desires. For our purposes, we shall speak of three types of situations from among this group. They correspond roughly to the psychological mechanisms known as "decomposition," "condensation," and *Verneinung*, or "denial."[5] In the case of decomposition, the semantic content of one proposition is conveyed by more than one arrangement of significant elements resembling a proposition. Some part of the original proposition is repeated in each of the resulting arrangements, while some part is changed. For example, the information conveyed by a sentence of the form: "X Yed Z." might be conveyed by a group of "apparent" sentences of the form: "A Yed Z; B Yed Z." or of the form: "A Yed U; B Yed V." or of the form: "X Med Z: Z Ned Z," etc. Where condensation is concerned, the semantic content of more than one proposition is conveyed by an arrangement of significant units resembling a single proposition. Parts of the original propositions are merged in parts of the resulting one. Thus, a set of sentences of the form: "A Yed Z; B Yed Z." is replaced by a sentence of the form: "X Yed Z," etc. Finally, in the case of *Verneinung*, one proposition is replaced simply by its negation. That is, a sentence of the form: "X Yed Z." is replaced by a sentence of the form: "X did not Y Z."

It must be emphasized that, although grammatical replacement arrangements of significant elements have "apparent meanings," these meanings are to be discounted. They are not to be understood in a "normal" or "linguistic" way. Thus, it becomes possible for grammatical arrangements of significant elements resembling complete, grammatical sentences to contain more or less information than any given logically complete proposition. We shall attempt to illustrate the functioning of these mechanisms in our discussion of the construction of Tragic Plots. For the moment, however, we must pursue some implications of the present discussion.

Undoubtedly, the most disturbing problem posed by the notion of the intelligible but obscured expression of information in works of art concerns the way in which the individual goes about distinguishing between the intended and apparent meanings of the arrangements of significant elements he perceives in the work. In order for the beholder to know that he is dealing with a work of art, he must be given various cues. In some cases, the conventionalized presentation of an object will be a clue to its character; we go to theaters, museums, and concert halls knowing we will perceive works of art there. Because the artist cannot count on such a factor, however, he must incorporate some device into his work signaling that it is a work of art. It is our contention that this device usually involves the artist's expressing himself in terms superficially so banal as to be quite uninteresting. That is, as a part of "seducing" the beholder into unraveling the meanings of obscured expressions, the artist presents him with something uninteresting that he can transform into something much more interesting. The emergence of the contemporary notion of "relevance" is but one piece of evidence

in favor of this claim, for, in fact, works of art are full of statements about things apparently too foreign to us to touch
us—the deaths of kings, sugar-plum fairies, shepherds tending
their flocks, etc. If we wish to obtain any important aesthetic
effect from the perception of works of art, we are obliged to
look beyond the superficial meanings of these statements.[6] Finally, once the beholder of an object containing intelligible expressions of information is cued to the fact that he is dealing
with a work of art and that he must go about understanding it in
a different way from the way he goes about understanding a
newspaper article or a textbook, he must rely on what we have
called a psychological performance model for understanding information contained in works of art.

2,iii. Mimesis and Symbolism

In order for the artist to communicate with the beholder of the
work of art, the psychological model he uses in expressing the
information contained in his work must be the same one as that
which the beholder uses in understanding it. This model is not a
conventional one, for the artist and the beholder do not consciously agree on a set of rules for interpreting the informational
content of any given work. We posit, to the contrary, that it is an
a priori model, similar to the one according to which the logical
categories of so-called natural languages are identified. It may be
thought of in terms of "innate," universal, human predispositions
to express and to understand certain kinds of information in certain ways under certain circumstances. In our discussion of
tragedy, we shall attempt to illustrate the functioning of a psychological performance model for the understanding of information contained in tragedies; we shall call what is described by
this model the "writer-spectator's intuition concerning the
tragic." What is important here, however, is simply that it is the
"procedures" for expressing and understanding this information
that represent universals, in aesthetic situations. That is to say,
only these procedures and the desires to be repressed represent

universals in these situations. It is in this context that we can speak of mimesis as a necessary part of the "construction" of a work of art.

It should be obvious that any conception of mimesis as the imitation or representation, in explicit terms, of "normal" or "probable" characters, actions, or situations is totally inadequate. One does not meet a Hercules or a Siegfried every day in the street, nor does one hear of parricides, of incests, or even of saintly acts very often. On the other hand, mimesis can reasonably be conceived as an imitation of some sort of "physis," i.e., a natural process. We maintain that the artist, in "painlessly" expressing information concerning the accomplishment of ungratifiable desires, "imitates," so to speak, the natural psychological process by which the beholder of the work of art goes about "painlessly" understanding such information. It is in this sense that works of art can and must be mimetic. It should be noted that no mimesis is involved in portraying the accomplishment of ungratifiable desires. Precisely because these desires are ungratifiable, the artist has no grounds for imitation. On the contrary, the artist always poses the accomplishment of ungratifiable desires as possible but inactual. Finally, we posit that the ways the artist suggests for accomplishing desires (which are the same as those the desirer believes will be effective) are exactly those allowed by his psychological performance model.

In so far as the application of the rules of a psychological performance model involve the replacement of some expressions by other expressions, the process may be thought of as involving symbolism. We take symbols to be no more than significant things that replace other significant things. They are *"signifiants"* that replace other *"signifiants."* It must be emphasized that they never signify the *"signifiants"* they replace; rather, they signify the *"signifié's"* already signified by these replaced *"signifiants."*[7] Furthermore, symbols must be functionally equivalent to the things they replace. Thus, for example, if a set of elements functionally replaces some significant element, then no one member of that set can be said to be symbolic of the replaced element; rather the set, as a whole, is symbolic of that element. Accordingly, the sets of sentences resulting from "decompositions," for instance, may be said to be symbolic of some original sentence. Similarly, all of the "actors" derived from some single "actant"[8] may be said collectively to symbolize that actant. These points will be illustrated in later discussions.

2,iv. Conclusion

In this chapter and in the preceding one, we have advanced various working hypotheses. We have introduced these hypotheses as summarily as possible, in order to avoid excessively long digressions on the many artistic, psychological, and philosophical problems a full justification of them might raise. To recapitulate, we have posited that the pleasure evoked by perceptions of tragic works is associated with the production of a state of belief. This state of belief is the result of understanding information, and the information understood constitutes what we have called tragic myth. Tragic myth can be resumed in a single abstract proposition: "A mythical self-annihilator annihilates himself with an instrument of self-annihilation," but the information contained in this proposition can be expressed concretely in whole sets of propositions called Tragic Plots. Finally, Tragic Plots are necessarily "obscure" expressions of the information constituting tragic myth. In the following chapter, we shall present a formal description of the ways in which this information is "obscured." This formal description is based on an empirical investigation of a well established corpus. Thus, if the explanatory hypotheses presented to this point seem highly speculative, the obvious predictive power of the descriptive component of our theory should lend them some credence.

Chapter Three

A Grammar of Tragic Myth

3,i. The Writer-Spectator's Intuition and the Understanding of Tragic Myth

We have introduced the notion of a "writer-spectator's intuition," a human faculty for creating and/or appreciating the tragic in tragic works of art. To create and to appreciate the tragic, the writer-spectator must be able to "perform" the operations involved in understanding aesthetically effective expressions of the essential tragic myth of self-annihilation. The performance of these operations can be described formally by a system of rules charting the process of understanding tragic myth. Such a system of rules constitutes a "psychological performance model." Whereas the rules of a performance model specify actions, the rules of a grammar specify possibilities for action. Thus, a grammar of tragic myth is a description of the possibilities for expressing and understanding tragic myth and not an account of the actual psychological activity of doing so. The anthropological interest of the grammar of tragic myth to be presented here lies in its paralleling a (hypothetical) performance model describing some genuine human activity, viz., the creation and appreciation of tragedies. Finally, the grammar of tragic myth, while not in itself a formal theory of the tragic genre, represents the heart of such a theory, for it characterizes the tangible phenomena that can generically be called tragedies, in view of their common aesthetic effects. In other words, although such a grammar does not account for such artisitic categories as "Diction" and "Spectacle," for example, it does detail the possibilities for expressing and understanding the specifically tragic in tragic works of art.

3,ii. The Scope of the Grammar of Tragic Myth

What is expressed in tragic myth is the act of self-annihilation. As we shall see, this act belongs to the class of Plot actions, for it is a transitive relation involving instruments.[1] In this sense, the grammar of tragic myth is a grammar of the structure of Tragic Plots. For theoretical purposes, we must distinguish between "Tragic Plots" and the "Plots of tragedies." Whereas the whole of tragic myth is expressed in the Plot of any given tragedy, the whole of the Plot of any given tragedy is not necessarily involved in expressing tragic myth. In other words, an adequate grammar of tragic myth, i.e., of Tragic Plots, is not necessarily an adequate grammar of the (overall) Plots of tragedies. The grammar of tragic myth proposes necessary but not sufficient criteria for characterizing these Plots. From an aesthetic point of view, only the information contained in the Tragic Plot is directly involved in the production of tragic pleasure, the other informational and noninformational aspects of any tragedy being of secondary importance.

The basic conceptual units of Tragic Plot structure, including specific character-types, actions, and instruments, collectively constitute what we shall call the "lexicon" of tragic myth. In compiling this lexicon, we have proceeded inductively from a consideration of the following corpus:

Sophocles: *Antigone, Electra, Oedipus Rex, The Women of Trachis*

Shakespeare: *Antony and Cleopatra, Coriolanus, Hamlet, Julius Caesar, King Lear, The Life and Death of King John, Macbeth, Othello, Richard II, Richard III, Romeo and Juliet, Timon of Athens, Titus Andronicus*

Racine: *Andromaque, Bajazet, Britannicus, Mithridate, Phèdre, La Thébaïde*[2] i.e., the tragic works of the leading dramatic authors of three major Occidental literary traditions. Obviously, this corpus is far from complete, and, consequently, it is probable that our lexicon is somewhat abridged. Its completion, however, is a practical matter depending solely on the investigation of an increasing number of other tragedies, and this incompleteness is of no particular theoretical importance. In fact, it will become clear that the tragic lexicon comprises a potentially infinite set of conceptual units whose number and presence in any given tragedy are limited only by considerations of memory and attention on the part of the writer-spectator.

The rules for combining the lexical units of tragic myth constitute the grammar of tragic myth. We cannot hope to present here the whole of this grammar, for, to be exhaustive, it must contain almost as many rules as there are tragedies. Moreover, the rules presented here will naturally require eventual refinements and modifications. The primary task at this stage is to propose a conceptual framework for the study of Tragic Plot structure, without attempting prematurely to give a definitive account. We shall present and explain only the major regularities in Tragic Plot structure, i.e., those that characterize the Tragic Plots of all tragedies; we shall leave the discovery of minor grammatical rules necessary for characterizing the Tragic Plots of individual tragedies to special investigations of these tragedies or of limited classes of them.

It must be emphasized that our grammar is based on a hypothetical performance model for expressing and understanding tragic myth. In this sense, the grammar must describe anthropologically interesting, i.e., human, potentials for performing the psychological and artistic operations involved in the creation and appreciation of tragic works. We postulate that the major regularities of Tragic Plot structure detailed in the grammar indicate major regularities in the human imaginative processes described by psychologists and, especially, by psychoanalysts, in their studies of dream, myth, art, and other symbolic systems, whereas the minor regularities of Tragic Plot structure illustrate the artistic processes described by "critics" in their studies of individual and/or traditional styles. In short, the general grammar of tragic myth presented here should satisfy the criterion already mentioned of adaptability; it should provide a basis for formalizing both psychological and artistic theories. Once the basic grammar has been specified, we shall discuss some of its major psychological, artistic, and philosophical implications.

3,iii. The Form of the Grammar of Tragic Myth

The grammar of Tragic Plot aims at formalizing the multitudinous possibilities for expressing and understanding the informational content of a fundamental proposition, a basic Plot sentence: "A (mythical) self-annihilator annihilates himself with an instrument of self-annihilation." The grammar of tragic myth must show how the whole of the Tragic Plot of any given tragedy can express all and only the information contained in this sentence. It must detail the possibilities for transforming the single "kernel-type" sentence into complex Tragic Plots and vice-versa. These possibilities can be described by a set of rules that, applied in a certain way, permit us to "derive" all potential Tragic Plots from the basic sentence given above or to trace them back to it.[3]

The rules of the grammar of tragic myth are all of one basic type. In the terminology of generative grammarians, they are "rewrite rules." They describe the possibilities for transforming one "string" of mythical elements into another and are of the general form: $X \rightarrow Y$, where the arrow is to be read: "can be rewritten as," or "can be transformed into." Among the rewrite rules of the grammar, subtypes can be distinguished on the basis of three major criteria:

(1) whether or not the rule provides for the decomposition of an abstract category into two or more subcategories,

(2) whether or not the rule provides for alternative derivations of abstract categories into mutually exclusive subcategories, and

(3) whether or not the rule stipulates that alternative derivations are possible only under certain conditions.

Rules that provide for the decomposition of abstract categories into subcategories will be called "multiplicational rules," whereas rules that do not provide for decompositions will be called "lexical rules." Rules that provide for alternative derivations of abstract categories will be said to involve "options." Finally, rules that stipulate that certain options can only be exploited under certain circumstances will be called "context-sensitive rules."

Rules with options will take the general form: A → X/Y/Z, where the slanted line is to be read "or" and the arrow to be read "can be rewritten as." Lexical rules with options take the general form: A → X/Y/Z, and the symbols X, Y, and Z always indicate simple, i.e. single, nonparenthesized units. On the other hand, multiplicational rules with options take the general form: A → X/Y/Z, but the symbols X, Y, and Z always stand for complex, i.e., multiple, parenthesized units. Thus, multiplicational rules with options take the specific form: A → (B + C)/(D + E)/(B + C + C)/(B + C + C + . . . C), etc. It will become clear that lexical rules provide for the replacement of single propositions by other single propositions, whereas multiplicational rules provide for the replacement of single propositions by two or more propositions.

Context-sensitive rules (all of which provide for options) account for the following possibilities:

(1) a certain option or set of options must be exploited under given circumstances;

(2) a certain option or set of options can never be exploited under given circumstances;

(3) a certain option or set of options can be exploited under any circumstances.

These rules take the general form: A → X (in the environment . . . PXQ) / Y (except in the environment . . . YRS . . .) / Z (. . . indicates an indeterminately long string of symbols of any nature). Finally, context-sensitive rules may be either lexical or multiplicational.

3,iv. Conventions for Applying the Rules of the Grammar

The rules of the grammar of tragic myth are to be applied in certain ways. First, they are to be applied in a fixed order. Rule 1 is to be applied to the initial "kernel-sentence-type" string of tragic myth; Rule 2 is to be applied to the string(s) resulting from the application of Rule 1, etc.

Second, rules will be applied two or more times consecutively to strings containing two or more symbols to which they can be applied. Each application of a rule is independent of every other application of that rule, and, in the case of rules with options, all of the options provided for by the rule remain open at each application. For example, a rule of the form: X → A/B/C, when applied to the string: XDXEXF, may yield a string of the form: ADXEXF, then a string of the form: ADCEXF, then a string of the form: ADCEAF. The first application of a rule will always be concerned with the first symbol in a string to which it can be applied, and each successive application will proceed towards the right. Finally, all of the symbols that can be transformed by the application of a rule must be transformed before one proceeds to the next rule.

Third, all complex, i.e., parenthesized, expressions in strings resulting from the application of given rules must be reduced algebraically before one proceeds to the application of further rules. This convention concerns multiplicational rules. By applying a rule of the form: X → (A + B) to a string of the form: XYZ, one would obtain a string of the form: (A + B)YZ. This string must be "worked out" to give the string: AYZ ; BYZ. The symbol ";" will be used here instead of the symbol "+" and will be read as the conjunction "and." In other words, the symbol ";" marks sentence boundaries within strings. It is a mark of the decomposition of single sentences into sets of sentences through the application of multiplicational rules.

Fourth, where the symbol "O" appears in a sentence contained in a string, that sentence is "voided." That is, that sentence, but not the whole string, loses any value as a means of expressing the information involved in constituting tragic myth. For reasons that we shall explain later, whole strings are voided when the symbol "O" is the only one preceeding any one or more of the symbols "M_1," "M_2," or "F." The voiding of strings and parts of strings is necessary for descriptive adequacy. Whereas early rules describe relatively general and abstract imaginative processes, voiding rules describe the limitations in realizing, in concrete form, various abstract possibilities.

Finally, we shall present both the rules of the grammar and any derivational examples in the form of formulae. These formulae consist of "strings" of symbols representing abstract categories in the structure of Tragic Plot generation and signs indicating the ways in which these strings are to be read or transformed. Since the grammar seeks to transform an initial string that is readable as a complete sentence, the other strings that will be generated by applying its rules will also be readable as complete sentences or sets of sentences. Consequently, Tragic Plots, when generated, should be readable as sets of complete sentences. The symbols used in the presentation of the rules of the grammar are noted below:

$\rightarrow$ "can be rewritten as"

$+$ *This sign has no reading. It appears only in parenthesized expressions and disappears when these expressions are worked out algebraically.*

$(\ )$ *This sign has no reading. It indicates that the elements contained inside it form an algebraic unit to be worked out by multiplication.*

;   *end of a sentence within a string*

.   *end of complete string*

/   *"or"*

,   *same as /, but used in context-sensitive rules to indicate options susceptible to the same conditions*

. . .   *a string of elements of undetermined nature or length. This symbol will be used primarily in context-sensitive rules to indicate an environment.*

MSA   *"Mythical Self-Annihilator"*

A   *"Annihilates"*

ISA   *"with an instrument of self-annihilation"*

H   *"Hero" ("Accomplishing Subject")*

D   "Desirer"
LA   "Legal Authority"
DO   "Desired Object"
M_1 "Illegal Obtainer"
M_2 "Initial Possessor"
F   "Object of desire and possession"
M_1' "Functional Partner of M_1"
M_2' "Functional partner of M_2"
F'   "Functional partner of F"
O   null sign, from which no further subcategories will be derived

In summary, the grammar of tragic myth is a model, constituted by rules describing the possibilities for transforming the
"kernel" Plot sentence containing the information necessary for
the production of tragic pleasure into sets of sentences containing the same information and constituting the Tragic Plots of
existing or possible tragedies. The application of each rule of the
grammar results in the production of a derived form of the initial
tragic myth sentence, and the steps involved in the elaboration
of a Tragic Plot from this initial sentence may be called, collectively, the "derivation" of that Tragic Plot. In the following sections, we shall attempt to explain and to illustrate the functioning
of the grammar of tragic myth. Having established the grammatical system, in its unavoidably abstract form, we shall proceed to demonstrate the development of an actual Tragic Plot
using the rules posited.

3,v. The Rules of the Grammar of Tragic Myth

The following rules are designed to serve in generating complete Tragic Plots from the sentence: "A mythical self-annihilator
annihilates himself with an instrument of self-annihilation." Thus,
the initial string on which the first rule of the grammar will oper-
ate is represented in the following way: MSA A MSA ISA. This
string is the initial string in the generation of all Tragic Plots.

Rule 1

MSA → H (in the environment A MSA ISA.) / (D + LA + DO) (in the
  environment MSA A ISA).

or, in ordinary language translation:

Mythical Self-Annihilator → Hero (when it precedes "Annihilates", etc.)
    / (Desirer + Legal Authority + Desired Object) (when it follows
    "Mythical Self-Annihilator Annihilates" and precedes "with an
    instrument of self-annihilation").

Application of Rule 1

Rule 1 is applied twice, because there are two MSAs in the
initial string: MSA A MSA ISA. The first application of Rule 1 to
this string yields the string:

H   A   MSA   ISA.
Hero Annihilates Mythical Self-Annihilator with an instrument of self-
                                                        annihilation.

The second application of Rule 1 yields the string:

H   A   (D   + LA   + DO   ISA.
Hero Annihilates (Desirer + Legal Authority + Desired Object) with an
                                    instrument of self-annihilation.

Before Rule 2 can apply, the parenthesized expression: (D + LA
+ DO) must be worked out. When this expression is worked
out, the resulting string is of the form:

H   A   D   ISA;
Hero Annihilates Desirer with an instrument of self-annihilation;

H   A   LA   ISA.
Hero Annihilates Legal Authority with an instrument of self-annihilation;

H   A   DO   ISA.
Hero Annihilates Desired Object with an instrument of self-annihilation.

Rule 1 provides for the imaginative "decomposition" of the
ideal mythical figure "MSA" into four functional categories. In
imagining himself as the microcosm in which the processes of
desiring and gratification take place, the "consumer-producer"

of tragedies must conceive the conflict ending these processes in terms of four principles. First, he must identify objects of desire, which, as objects, may be either animate or inanimate. (It will become clear that the derivatives of the category DO [Desired Object] may be represented as human or nonhuman objects.) Second, the individual must identify a desiring principle, i.e., a desirer, who, in his capacity as a desirer, must be animate; that is, as the subject of the transitive relation of desiring, the desirer can only be represented by human "characters." Third, he must identify an authoritative principle or legal authority. This principle is reflected in the category LA (Legal Authority), which must also be represented by animate derivatives. Finally, the individual must identify an accomplishing principle, one that brings about the gratification of the desirer's desire by nullifying the legal authority and the desired quality of the desired object. In other words, the Hero or Accomplishing Subject effectively destroys the desirer by ending his desiring, the legal authority by overcoming its authority, i.e., its power, and the desired object by changing its quality from desired to possessed. Naturally, the heroic function can only be represented by animate derivatives.

If one opposes the necessarily animate categories (H, D, and LA) of the writer-spectator's psychological microcosm to the one remaining category (DO) which is not necessarily animate, one has a formal basis for distinguishing the "personality" from the intentionally constituted "external world," whose conceptual structure necessitates the fragmentation of the personality into three functional principles. On the other hand, it will become clear presently that there is some functional overlapping between the "personality principles" and the "desired principle." For this reason, the intentionally constituted external world of concepts is to be considered as much a part of the psychological microcosm indicated by the category MSA as the personality. With regard to the three "personality principles" mentioned above, the roles of the categories H, D, and LA should be obvious. They correspond quite neatly to the psychoanalytic categories of the ego, the id, and the superego, respectively.

However, the category H assumes all of the active aspects of the id and the superego, while the categories D and LA assume all of their passive aspects, as well as all the aspects of the ego.[4] Rules 2–5 will illustrate this point in formal ways.

Rule 2
(in symbolic form):

$$H \rightarrow (M_1 + M_1')/(M_1 + M_1' + M_1')/(M_1 + M_1' + M_1' + \ldots M_1')/(M_2 + M_2')/(M_2 + M_2' + M_2')/(M_2 + M_2' + M_2' + \ldots M_2')/(F + F')/(F + F' + F')/(F + F' + F' + \ldots F').[5]$$

(in ordinary language translation);

Hero →(Illegal Obtainer + Functional partner of Illegal Obtainer)/

(Illegal Obtainer + Functional partner of Illegal Obtainer + Functional partner of Illegal Obtainer)/

(Illegal Obtainer + Functional partner of Illegal Obtainer + Functional partner of Illegal Obtainer + . . . (an undetermined number of functional partners of Illegal Obtainer) Functional partner of Illegal Obtainer)/

(Initial Possessor + Functional partner of Initial Possessor)/

(Initial Possessor + Functional partner of Initial Possessor + Functional partner of Initial Possessor)/

(Initial Possessor + Functional partner of Initial Possessor + Functional partner of Initial Possessor + . . . (an undetermined number of functional partners of Initial Possessor) Functional partner of Initial Possessor)/

(Object of desire and possession + Functional partner of Object of desire and possession)/

(Object of desire and possession + Functional partner of Object of desire and possession + Functional partner of Object of desire and possession)/

(Object of desire and possession + Functional partner of Object of desire and possession + Functional partner of Object of desire and possession + . . . (an undetermined number of functional partners of Object of desire and possession) Functional partner of Object of desire and possession).

Rule 2 is a multiplicational rule with options. It provides for the decomposition of the category H into sets of categories, involving a central "actant" and its functional partner(s), at any point at which it occurs. Since it occurs in three places in the string resulting from the application of Rule 1, there are three occasions for multiplying the number of sentences in that string an indeterminately great number of times. We cannot hope to present all of the possible "outputs" of Rule 2. However, we can practically present the full range of possibilities indicated by Rule 2 that involve choosing optional derivatives of the category H containing only one "Functional partner." The alternative strings resulting from the applications of Rule 2 are (in symbolic form):

1) M_1 A D ISA; M_1' A D ISA, M_1 A LA ISA; M_1' A LA ISA; M_1 A DO ISA; M_1' A DO ISA.

2) M_1 A D ISA; M_1' A D ISA; M_2 A LA ISA; M_2' A LA ISA; M_1 A DO ISA; M_1' A DO ISA.

3) M_1 A D ISA; M_1' A D ISA; M_1 A LA ISA; M_1' A LA ISA; M_2 A DO ISA; M_2' A DO ISA.

4) M_1 A D ISA; M_1' A D ISA: M_2 A LA ISA; M_2' A LA ISA; M_2 A DO ISA; M_2' A DO ISA.

5) M_1 A D ISA; M_1' A D ISA; F A LA ISA; F' A LA ISA; M_1 A DO ISA; M_1' A DO ISA.

6) M_1 A D ISA; M_1' A D ISA; M_1 A LA ISA; M_1' A LA ISA; F A DO ISA; F' A DO ISA.

7) M_1 A D ISA; M_1' A D ISA; F A LA ISA; F' A LA ISA; F A DO ISA; F' A DO ISA.

8) M_1 A D ISA; M_1' A D ISA; M_2 A LA ISA; M_2' A LA ISA; F A DO ISA; F' A DO ISA.

9) M_1 A D ISA; M_1' A D ISA; F A LA ISA; F' A LA ISA; M_2 A DO ISA; M_2' A DO ISA.

10) M_2 A D ISA; M_2' A D ISA; M_2 A LA ISA; M_2' A LA ISA: M_2 A DO ISA; M_2' A DO ISA.

11) M_2 A D ISA; M_2' A D ISA; M_1 A LA ISA; M_1' A LA ISA; M_2 A DO ISA; M_2' A DO ISA.

12) M_2 A D ISA; M_2' A D ISA; M_2 A LA ISA; M_2' A LA ISA; M_1 A DO ISA; M_1' A DO ISA.

13) M_2 A D ISA; M_2' A D ISA; M_1 A LA ISA; M_1' A LA ISA; M_1 A DO ISA; M_1' A DO ISA.

14) M_2 A D ISA; M_2' A D ISA; F A LA ISA; F' A LA ISA; M_2 A DO ISA; M_2' A DO ISA.

15) M_2 A D ISA; M_2' A D ISA; M_2 A LA ISA; M_2' A LA ISA; F A DO ISA; F' A DO ISA.

16) M_2 A D ISA: M_2' A D ISA: F A LA ISA; F' A LA ISA; F A DO ISA; F' A DO ISA.

17) M_2 A D ISA; M_2' A D ISA; M_1 A LA ISA; M_1' A LA ISA; F A DO ISA; F' A DO ISA.

18) M_2 A D ISA; M_2' A D ISA; F A LA ISA; F' A LA ISA; M_1 A DO ISA; M_1' A DO ISA.

19) F A D ISA; F' A D ISA; F A LA ISA; F' A LA ISA; F A DO ISA; F' A DO ISA.

20) F A D ISA; F' A D ISA; M_1 A LA ISA; M_1' A LA ISA; F A DO ISA; F' A DO ISA.

21) F A D ISA; F' A D ISA; F A LA ISA; F' A LA ISA; M_1 A DO ISA; M_1' A DO ISA.

22) F A D ISA; F' A D ISA; M_1 A LA ISA; M_1' A LA ISA; M_1 A DO ISA; M_1' A DO ISA.

23) F A D ISA; F' A D ISA; M_2 A LA ISA; M_2' A LA ISA; F A DO ISA; F' A DO ISA.

24) F A D ISA; F' A D ISA; F A LA ISA; F' A LA ISA; M_2 A DO ISA; M_2' A DO ISA.

25) F A D ISA; F' A D ISA; M_2 A LA ISA; M_2' A LA ISA; M_2 A DO ISA; M_2' A DO ISA.

26) F A D ISA; F' A D ISA; M_1 A LA ISA; M_1' A LA ISA: M_2 A DO ISA; M_2' A DO ISA.

27) F A D ISA; F' A D ISA; M_2 A LA ISA; M_2' A LA ISA; M_1 A DO ISA; M_1' A DO ISA.

and, in ordinary language translation:

1) Illegal Obtainer Annihilates Desirer with an instrument of self-annihilation; Functional partner of Illegal Obtainer Annihilates Desirer with an instrument of self-annihilation; Illegal Obtainer Annihilates Legal Authority with an instrument of self-annihilation; Functional partner of Illegal Obtainer Annihilates Legal Authority with an instrument of self-annihilation; Illegal Obtainer Annihilates Desired Object with an instrument of self-annihilation; Functional partner of Illegal Obtainer Annihilates Desired Object with an instrument of self-annihilation.

2) Illegal Obtainer Annihilates Desirer with an instrument of self-annihilation; Functional partner of Illegal Obtainer Annihilates Desirer with an instrument of self-annihilation; Initial Possessor Annihilates Legal Authority with an instrument of self-annihilation; Functional partner of Initial Possessor Annihilates Legal Authority with an instrument of self-annihilation; Illegal Obtainer Annihilates Desired Object with an instrument of self-annihilation; Functional partner of Illegal Obtainer Annihilates Desired Object with an instrument of self-annihilation.

3) Illegal Obtainer Annihilates Desirer with an instrument of self-annihilation; Functional partner of Illegal Obtainer Annihilates Desirer with an instrument of self-annihilation; Illegal Obtainer Annihilates Legal Authority with an instrument of self-annihilation; Functional partner of Illegal Obtainer Annihilates Legal Authority with an instrument of self-annihilation; Initial Possessor Annihilates Desired Object with an instrument of self-annihilation; Functional partner of Initial Possessor Annihilates Desired Object with an instrument of self-annihilation.

4) Illegal Obtainer Annihilates Desirer with an instrument of self-annihilation; Functional partner of Illegal Obtainer Annihilates Desirer with an instrument of self-annihilation; Initial Possessor Annihilates Legal Authority with an instrument of self-annihilation; Functional partner of Initial Possessor Annihilates Legal Authority with an instrument of self-annihilation; Initial Possessor Annihilates Desired Object with an instrument of self-annihilation; Functional partner of Initial Possessor Annihilates Desired Object with an instrument of self-annihilation.

5) Illegal Obtainer Annihilates Desirer with an instrument of self-annihilation; Functional partner of Illegal Obtainer Annihilates Desirer with an instrument of self-annihilation; Desired Object Annihilates Legal Authority with an instrument of self-annihilation; Functional partner of Desired Object Annihilates Legal Authority with an instrument of self-annihilation; Illegal Obtainer Annihilates Desired Object with an instrument of self-annihilation; Functional partner of Illegal Obtainer Annihilates Desired Object with an instrument of self-annihilation.

6) Illegal Obtainer Annihilates Desirer with an instrument of self-annihilation; Functional partner of Illegal Obtainer Annihilates Desirer with an instrument of self-annihilation; Illegal Obtainer Annihilates Legal Authority with an instrument of self-annihilation; Functional partner of Illegal Obtainer Annihilates Legal Authority with an instrument of self-annihilation; Object of desire and possession Annihilates Desired Object with an instrument of self-annihilation; Functional partner of Object of desire and possession Annihilates Desired Object with an instrument of self-annihilation.

7) Illegal Obtainer Annihilates Desirer with an instrument of self-annihilation; Functional partner of Illegal Obtainer Annihilates Desirer with an instrument of self-annihilation; Object of desire and possession Annihilates Legal Authority with an instrument of self-annihilation; Functional partner of Object of desire and possession Annihilates Legal Authority with an instrument of self-annihilation; Object of desire and possession Annihilates Desired Object with an instrument of self-annihilation; Functional partner of Object of desire and possession Annihilates Desired Object with an instrument of self-annihilation.

8) Illegal Obtainer Annihilates Desirer with an instrument of self-annihilation; Functional partner of Illegal Obtainer Annihilates Desirer with an instrument of self-annihilation; Initial Possessor Annihilates Legal Authority with an instrument of self-annihilation; Functional partner of Initial Possessor Annihilates Legal Authority with an instrument of self-annihilation; Object of desire and possession Annihilates Desired Object with an instrument of self-annihilation; Functional partner of Object of desire and possession Annihilates Desired Object with an instrument of self-annihilation.

9) Illegal Obtainer Annihilates Desirer with an instrument of self-annihilation; Functional partner of Illegal Obtainer Annihilates Desirer with an instrument of self-annihilation; Object of desire and possession Annihilates Legal Authority with an instrument of self-annihilation; Functional partner of Object of desire and possession Annihilates Legal Authority with an instrument of self-annihilation; Initial Possessor Annihilates Desired Object with an instrument of self-annihilation; Functional partner of Initial Possessor Annihilates Desired Object with an instrument of self-annihilation.

10) Initial Possessor Annihilates Desirer with an instrument of self-annihilation; Functional partner of Initial Possessor Annihilates Desirer with an instrument of self-annihilation; Initial Possessor Annihilates Legal Authority with an instrument of self-annihilation; Functional part-

ner of Initial Possessor Annihilates Legal Authority with an instrument of self-annihilation; Initial Possessor Annihilates Desired Object with an instrument of self-annihilation; Functional partner of Initial Possessor Annihilates Desired Object with an instrument of self-annihilation.

11) Initial Possessor Annihilates Desirer with an instrument of self-annihilation; Functional partner of Initial Possessor Annihilates Desirer with an instrument of self-annihilation; Illegal Obtainer Annihilates Legal Authority with an instrument of self-annihilation; Functional partner of Illegal Obtainer Annihilates Legal Authority with an instrument of self-annihilation; Initial Possessor Annihilates Desired Object with an instrument of self-annihilation; Functional partner of Initial Possessor Annihilates Desired Object with an instrument of self-annihilation.

12) Initial Possessor Annihilates Desirer with an instrument of self-annihilation; Functional partner of Initial Possessor Annihilates Desirer with an instrument of self-annihilation; Initial Possessor Annihilates Legal Authority with an instrument of self-annihilation; Functional partner of Initial Possessor Annihilates Legal Authority with an instrument of self-annihilation; Illegal Obtainer Annihilates Desired Object with an instrument of self-annihilation; Functional partner of Illegal Obtainer Annihilates Desired Object with an instrument of self-annihilation.

13) Initial Possessor Annihilates Desirer with an instrument of self-annihilation; Functional partner of Initial Possessor Annihilates Desirer with an instrument of self-annihilation; Illegal Obtainer Annihilates Legal Authority with an instrument of self-annihilation; Functional partner of Illegal Obtainer Annihilates Legal Authority with an instrument of self-annihilation; Illegal Obtainer Annihilates Desired Object with an instrument of self-annihilation; Functional partner of Illegal Obtainer Annihilates Desired Object with an instrument of self-annihilation.

14) Initial Possessor Annihilates Desirer with an instrument of self-annihilation; Functional partner of Initial Possessor Annihilates Desirer with an instrument of self-annihilation; Object of desire and possession Annihilates Legal Authority with an instrument of self-annihilation; Functional partner of Object of desire and possession Annihilates Legal Authority with an instrument of self-annihilation; Initial Possessor Annihilates Desired Object with an instrument of self-annihilation; Functional Partner of Initial Possessor Annihilates Desired Object with an instrument of self-annihilation.

15) Initial Possessor Annihilates Desirer with an instrument of self-annihilation; Functional partner of Initial Possessor Annihilates Desirer

with an instrument of self-annihilation; Initial Possessor Annihilates Legal Authority with an instrument of self-annihilation; Functional partner of Initial Possessor Annihilates Legal Authority with an instrument of self-annihilation; Object of desire and possession Annihilates Desired Object with an instrument of self-annihilation; Functional partner of Object of desire and possession Annihilates Desired Object with an instrument of self-annihilation.

16) Initial Possessor Annihilates Desirer with an instrument of self-annihilation; Functional partner of Initial Possessor Annihilates Desirer with an instrument of self-annihilation; Illegal Obtainer Annihilates Legal Authority with an instrument of self-annihilation; Functional partner of Illegal Obtainer Annihilates Legal Authority with an instrument of self-annihilation; Object of desire and possession Annihilates Desired Object with an instrument of self-annihilation; Functional partner of Object of desire and possession Annihilates Desired Object with an instrument of self-annihilation.

17) Initial Possessor Annihilates Desirer with an instrument of self-annihilation; Functional partner of Initial Possessor Annihilates Desirer with an instrument of self-annihilation; Object of desire and possession Annihilates Legal Authority with an instrument of self-annihilation; Functional partner of Object of desire and possession Annihilates Legal Authority with an instrument of self-annihilation; Illegal Obtainer Annihilates Desired Object with an instrument of self-annihilation; Functional partner of Illegal Obtainer Annihilates Desired Object with an instrument of self-annihilation.

18) Initial Possessor Annihilates Desirer with an Instrument of Self-Annihilation; Functional partner of Initial Possessor Annihilates Desirer with an Instrument of Self-Annihilation; Object of desire and possession Annihilates Legal Authority with an Instrument of Self-Annihilation; Functional partner of Object of desire and possession Annihilates Legal Authority with an Instrument of Self-Annihilation; Illegal Obtainer Annihilates Desired Object with an Instrument of Self-Annihilation; Functional partner of Illegal Obtainer Annihilates Desired Object with an Instrument of Self-Annihilation.

19) Object of desire and possession Annihilates Desirer with an instrument of self-annihilation; Functional partner of Object of desire and possession Annihilates Desirer with an instrument of self-annihilation; Object of desire and possession Annihilates Legal Authority with an instrument of self-annihilation; Functional partner of Object of desire and possession Annihilates Legal Authority with an instrument of self-

annihilation; Object of desire and possession Annihilates Desired Object with an instrument of self-annihilation; Functional partner of Object of desire and possession Annihilates Desired Object with an instrument of self-annihilation.

20) Object of desire and possession Annihilates Desirer with an instrument of self-annihilation; Functional partner of Object of desire and possession Annihilates Desirer with an instrument of self-annihilation; Illegal Obtainer Annihilates Legal Authority with an instrument of self-annihilation; Functional partner of Illegal Obtainer Annihilates Legal Authority with an instrument of self-annihilation; Object of desire and possession Annihilates Desired Object with an instrument of self-annihilation; Functional partner of Object of desire and possession Annihilates Desired Object with an instrument of self-annihilation.

21) Object of desire and possession Annihilates Desirer with an instrument of self-annihilation; Functional partner of Object of desire and possession Annihilates Desirer with an instrument of self-annihilation; Object of desire and possession Annihilates Legal Authority with an instrument of self-annihilation; Functional partner of Object of desire and possession Annihilates Legal Authority with an instrument of self-annihilation; Illegal Obtainer Annihilates Desired Object with an instrument of self-annihilation; Functional partner of Illegal Obtainer Annihilates Desired Object with an instrument of self-annihilation.

22) Object of desire and possession Annihilates Desirer with an instrument of self-annihilation; Functional partner of Object of desire and possession Annihilates Desirer with an instrument of self-annihilation; Illegal Obtainer Annihilates Legal Authority with an instrument of self-annihilation; Functional partner of Illegal Obtainer Annihilates Legal Authority with an instrument of self-annihilation; Illegal Obtainer Annihilates Desired Object with an instrument of self-annihilation; Functional partner of Illegal Obtainer Annihilates Desired Object with an instrument of self-annihilation.

23) Object of desire and possession Annihilates Desirer with an instrument of self-annihilation; Functional partner of Object of desire and possession Annihilates Desirer with an instrument of self-annihilation; Initial Possessor Annihilates Legal Authority with an instrument of self-annihilation; Functional partner of Initial Possessor Annihilates Legal Authority with an instrument of self-annihilation; Object of desire and possession Annihilates Desired Object with an instrument of self-annihilation; Functional partner of Object of desire and possession Annihilates Desired Object with an instrument of self-annihilation.

24) Object of desire and possession Annihilates Desirer with an instrument of self-annihilation; Functional partner of Object of desire and possession Annihilates Desirer with an instrument of self-annihilation; Object of desire and possession Annihilates Legal Authority with an instrument of self-annihilation; Functional partner of Object of desire and possession Annihilates Legal Authority with an instrument of self-annihilation; Initial Possessor Annihilates Desired Object with an instrument of self-annihilation; Functional partner of Initial Possessor Annihilates Desired Object with an instrument of self-annihilation.

25) Object of desire and possession Annihilates Desirer with an instrument of self-annihilation; Functional partner of Object of desire and possession Annihilates Desirer with an instrument of self-annihilation; Initial Possessor Annihilates Legal Authority with an instrument of self-annihilation; Functional partner of Initial Possessor Annihilates Legal Authority with an instrument of self-annihilation; Initial Possessor Annihilates Desired Object with an instrument of self-annihilation; Functional partner of Initial Possessor Annihilates Desired Object with an instrument of self-annihilation.

26) Object of desire and possession Annihilates Desirer with an instrument of self-annihilation; Functional partner of Object of desire and possession Annihilates Desirer with an instrument of self-annihilation; Illegal Obtainer Annihilates Legal Authority with an instrument of self-annihilation; Functional partner of Illegal Obtainer Annihilates Legal Authority with an instrument of self-annihilation; Initial Possessor Annihilates Desired Object with an instrument of self-annihilation; Functional partner of Initial Possessor Annihilates Desired Object with an instrument of self-annihilation.

27) Object of desire and possession Annihilates Desirer with an instrument of self-annihilation; Functional partner of Object of desire and possession Annihilates Desirer with an instrument of self-annihilation; Initial Possessor Annihilates Legal Authority with an instrument of self-annihilation; Functional partner of Initial Possessor Annihilates Legal Authority with an instrument of self-annihilation; Illegal Obtainer Annihilates Desired Object with an instrument of self-annihilation; Functional partner of Illegal Obtainer Annihilates Desired Object with an instrument of self-annihilation.

In other words, there are 27 (3^3) basic alternative string types indicated by Rule 2. We posit that choosing derivatives of the category (H) (Hero) containing more than one Functional partner does not change the fundamental character of any of these string types. After presenting Rules 3–5, we shall discuss the importance of these 27 alternative possibilities as a basis for a classification of Tragic Plot types. Such a discussion will best be presented after Rules 3–5, because the nature of the categories M_1, M_1', M_2, M_2', F, and F', will be clearest at that point. For the moment, however, it should suffice to point out that Rule 2 provides for the first options in the generation of Tragic Plots. Its application produces strings that do not figure in the derivations of all Tragic Plots. On the contrary, the appearance of any string from among the 27 types listed, in such a derivation, may be used to characterize the Tragic Plot in question as a member of a particular class.

Rule 3

D $(M_1$ $+ M_1')$
Desirer→(Illegal Obtainer + Functional partner of Illegal Obtainer)/

   $(M_1$ $+ M_1'$
   (Illegal Obtainer + Functional partner of Illegal Obtainer

   $+ M_1')$ $(M_1$
   + Functional partner of Illegal Obtainer)/(Illegal Obtainer

   $+ M_1'$
   + Functional partner of Illegal Obtainer

   $+ M_1'$
   + Functional partner of Illegal Obtainer

   $+ \ldots M_1'$
   $+ \ldots$ Functional partner of Illegal Obtainer).

Rule 4

LA $(M_2$
Legal Authority→(Initial Possessor

   $+ M_2'$ $(M_2$
   + Functional partner of Initial Possessor)/(Initial Possessor

   $+ M_2'$
   + Functional partner of Initial Possessor

+M$_2$')   (M$_2$
+ Functional partner of Initial Possessor)/(Initial Possessor

+ M$_2$'
+ Functional partner of Initial Possessor

+ M$_2$'
+ Functional partner of Initial Possessor

+ . . . M$_2$'
+ . . . Functional partner of Initial Possessor).

Rule 5

DO   (F
Desired Object→(Object of desire and possession

+ F')
+ Functional partner of Object of desire and possession)/

(F   + F'
(Object of desire and possession + Functional partner of Object
                                                of desire and possession

+ F')
+ Functional partner of Object of desire and possession)/

(F   + F'
(Object of desire and possession + Functional partner of Object
                                                of desire and possession

+F'
+ Functional partner of Object of desire and possession

+ . . . F')
+ . . . Functional partner of Object of desire and possession).

Rules 3–5 are multiplicational rules with options. Taking as an example the first optional string generated by Rule 2, we shall attempt to illustrate the operation of Rules 3–5. The string on which Rule 3 will apply is:

A) M$_1$ A   D   ISA;
   Illegal Obtainer Annihilates Desirer with an instrument of self-
                                                annihilation;

M₁'   A   D   ISA;
Functional partner of Illegal Obtainer Annihilates Desirer with an in-
                                        strument of self-annihilation;

M₁   A   LA   ISA;
Illegal Obtainer Annihilates Legal Authority with an instrument of
                                        self-annihilation;

M₁'   A   LA   ISA;
Functional partner of Illegal Obtainer Annihilates Legal Authority with
                              an instrument of self-annihilation;

M₁   A   DO   ISA;
Illegal Obtainer Annihilates Desired Object with an instrument of
                                        self-annihilation;

M₁   A   DO   ISA;
Functional partner of Illegal Obtainer Annihilates Desired Object with
                              an instrument of self-annihilation;

This string consists of six sentences. By applying Rule 3 and
choosing the first alternative provided by it, we obtain the basic
eight-sentence string:

B) M₁   A   M₁   ISA;
Illegal Obtainer Annihilates Illegal Obtainer with an instrument of
                                        self-annihilation;

M₁'   A   M₁   ISA;
Functional partner of Illegal Obtainer Annihilates Illegal Obtainer with
                              an instrument of self-annihilation;

M₁   A   M₁'   ISA;
Illegal Obtainer Annihilates Functional partner of Illegal Obtainer with
                              an instrument of self-annihilation;

M₁'   A   M₁'
Functional partner of Illegal Obtainer Annihilates Functional partner
                              ISA;
             of Illegal Obtainer with an instrument of self-annihilation;

M₁   A   LA   ISA;
Iilegal Obtainer Annihilates Legal Authority with an instrument of
                                        self-annihilation;

M₁'   A   LA   ISA;
Functional partner of Illegal Obtainer Annihilates Legal Authority with
                        an instrument of self-annihilation;

M₁   A   DO   ISA;
Illegal Obtainer Annihilates Desired Object with an instrument of
                                        self-annihilation;

M₁'   A   DO   ISA;
Functional partner of Illegal Obtainer Annihilates Desired Object with
an instrument of self-annihilation;

By applying Rule 4 and choosing the first alternative provided by
it, we obtain the ten-sentence string:

C) M₁   A   M₁   ISA;
Illegal Obtainer Annihilates Illegal Obtainer with an instrument of
                                        self-annihilation;

M₁'   A   M₁   ISA;
Functional partner of Illegal Obtainer Annihilates Illegal Obtainer with
                        an instrument of self-annihilation;

M₁   A   M₁'   ISA;
Illegal Obtainer Annihilates Functional partner of Illegal Obtainer with
                        an instrument of self-annihilation;

M₁'   A   M₁'
Functional partner of Illegal Obtainer Annihilates Functional partner
                        ISA;
        of Illegal Obtainer with an instrument of self-annihilation;

M₁   A   M₂   ISA;
Illegal Obtainer Annihilates Initial Possessor with an instrument of
                                        self-annihilation;

M₁'   A   M₂
Functional partner of Illegal Obtainer Annihilates Initial Possessor
                        ISA;
                        with an instrument of self-annihilation;

M₁   A   M₂'
Illegal Obtainer Annihilates Functional partner of Initial Possessor
                        ISA;
                        with an instrument of self-annihilation;

M₁′   A   M₂′
Functional partner of Illegal Obtainer Annihilates Functional partner
                          ISA;
     of Initial Possessor with an instrument of self-annihilation;

M₁   A   DO   ISA;
Illegal Obtainer Annihilates Desired Object with an instrument of
                                        self-annihilation;

M₁′   A   DO   ISA;
Functional partner of Illegal Obtainer Annihilates Desired Object with
an instrument of self-annihilation;

Finally, by applying Rule 5 and choosing the first alternative provided by it, we obtain the basic twelve-sentence string:

D) M₁   A   M₁   ISA;
   Illegal Obtainer Annihilates Illegal Obtainer with an instrument of
                                        self-annihilation;

M₁′   A   M₁   ISA;
Functional partner of Illegal Obtainer Annihilates Illegal Obtainer with
                          an instrument of self-annihilation;

M₁   A   M₁′   ISA
Illegal Obtainer Annihilates Functional partner of Illegal Obtainer with
                          an instrument of self-annihilation;

M₁′   A   M₁′
Functional partner of Illegal Obtainer Annihilates Functional partner
                          ISA;
     of Illegal Obtainer with an instrument of self-annihilation;

M₁   A   M₂   ISA;
Illegal Obtainer Annihilates Initial Possessor with an instrument of
                                        self-annihilation;

M₁′   A   M₂
Functional partner of Illegal Obtainer Annihilates Initial Possessor
                          ISA;
                          with an instrument of self-annihilation;

M₁   A   M₂′
Illegal Obtainer Annihilates Functional partner of Initial Possessor
                          ISA;
                          with an instrument of self-annihilation;

M_1' A M_2'
Functional partner of Illegal Obtainer Annihilates Functional partner
ISA;
    of Initial Possessor with an instrument of self-annihilation;

M_1 A   F   ISA;
Illegal Obtainer Annihilates Object of desire and possession with an
instrument of self-annihilation;

M_1' A   F
Functional partner of Illegal Obtainer Annihilates Object of desire
ISA;
    and possession with an instrument of self-annihilation;

M_1 A   F'
Illegal Obtainer Annihilates Functional partner of Object of desire
ISA;
    and possession with an instrument of self-annihilation;

M_1' A   F'
Functional partner of Illegal Obtainer Annihilates Functional partner
ISA;
of Object of desire and possession with an instrument of self-
annihilation;

Rules 3 through 5 are particularly interesting in that they rees-
tablish at least some of the symmetry of the initial "reflexive"
Plot sentence of tragic myth. That is, in strings resulting from
the application of Rule 5, all of the symbols that can appear immediately to the left of the symbol A can also appear immediately to the right of that symbol. Of course, as in the case
of string D above, the distribution of these symbols is not always
perfectly symmetrical. The function of Rule 2 is to scramble the
second derivatives of the category MSA on the left side of the
symbol A, while the function of Rules 3 through 5 is to expand
the first derivatives of the category MSA on the right side of the
symbol A. The categories to the right of the symbol A must be
kept distinct, because the act of self-annihilation is always imagined in terms of the destruction of three separate and distinct
principles. The way in which this destruction comes about, however, is subject to great imaginative flexibility. It is for this reason

that the symbols to the left of the symbol A can be scrambled. As we have said, the categories D, LA, and DO represent passive principles, two of whose derivatives must have and one of whose derivatives can have active aspects. The choice of "Accomplishing Subjects," or "heroic subactants" represented by the symbols to the left of the symbol A must be made from among these active aspects. In other words, the sets of symbols appearing to the left of the symbol A always correspond to one or more of the sets of symbols appearing to the right of that symbol.

Our choice of the symbols M and F is based on the distinction between the passive principles necessarily having active aspects and those not necessarily having active aspects, i.e., between D and LA on one side and DO on the other. M is an abbreviation for Masculine and F an abbreviation for Feminine, but it must be emphasized that these terms are meant in a grammatical, i.e. differential, and not in a sexual sense. In existing tragedies, the derivatives of the symbols M and F are invariably male and female characters, respectively, but we maintain that this situation is the result of the exclusively male authorship of these tragedies. That is, the male dramatist ordinarily imagines the class of "possessing" principles as male and the class of "possessed" principles as female. It may well be that the male spectator alone is susceptible to the understanding of such an imaginative process.[6] On the other hand, since the symbols M and F are generic and not sexual, their derivatives might, theoretically, be female and male characters, respectively. The theoretical possibility has simply never been exploited. Finally, although the patients in Tragic Plots are always divided into three groups two of which are represented by male characters and the third by female characters or certain types of inanimate objects, the agents in Tragic Plots may be all male, all female, or some combination of male and female characters. We shall attempt to explain why only some from among the 27 combinations of agents and patients generated by Rule 2 are ever actually exploited in existing tragedies.

The 27 string types resulting from the application of Rule 2 can be classified into groups of fundamental Plot Types. We can distinguish one set of strings whose exploitation in existing tragedies seems impossible, for fairly clear psychological reasons, one set of string types whose exploitation in existing tragedies seems possible, although they are unexploited (at least in the corpus on which this study is based), and one set of string types whose exploitation is both possible and actual.

Strings 3, 4, 9, 11, 14, 24, 25, and 26 are never exploited in generating Tragic Plots. They all have one thing in common which seems to render their exploitation impossible. That is, they all contain sentences of the form: M_2 A F ISA; M_2' A F ISA; M_2 A F' ISA, and M_2' A F' ISA. Given that M_2 and M_2' are the peculiar derivatives of the category LA and that F and F' are the peculiar derivatives of the category DO, it is understandable that the imagination does not conceive of the destruction of F and F' by M_2 and M_2'. It is only natural that the legal authority that one imagines as protecting the desired object not be imagined as destroying it. Of course, it must be noted that this reason is not absolute, as the case of string 10 will show. However, string 10 represents a very "explainable" exception, and we shall discuss its case below.

Strings 5, 7, 12, 16, 18, 20, 21, 22, 23, and 27 are, likewise, not exploited in existing tragedies. On the other hand, they do not seem totally impossible from an imaginative point of view. Here, the reasons for the nonexploitation of the strings in question are more varied and perhaps less compelling than in the case of those just mentioned. Strings 5, 7, 16, 18, and 21 have one thing in common. They all contain sentences in which derivatives of the category DO are seen to destroy derivatives of the category LA. In one sense, it does seem reasonable that a protected object would not destroy its protector. On the other hand, it also seems reasonable to assume that one might imagine a desired object as "cooperating" with the desirer, because the desirer's desire is projected onto the object. In any case, what we take to be a possibility is only realized in another very explainable exception, namely string 19, which we shall also discuss below. The imagined "nonaggression pact" between the derivatives of the categories LA and DO reflects an imaginative process noted by Melanie Klein and other psychoanalysts, in which the object and authority figures of the mother and the father are merged into one. We might add that the idea that one might imagine the desired object as cooperating with the desirer is also reflected in the nonaggression of the derivatives of the category DO on those of the category D. This nonaggression is illustrated by the nonexploitation of strings 20, 22, 23, and 27. Again, string 19 presents an explainable exception. Among the possible but unexploited cases, only that of string 12 remains. Here, we can only suggest that, where the derivatives of the category D are not assigned active aspects with respect to either of the two sets of isogeneric category derivatives, they are assigned none at all. This point may become clearer with further discussions. These appear to be the major reasons for the nonexploitation of various string types. There may, of course, be more adequate and/or more numerous reasons, but future investigations will have to discover them.

Having suggested some explanations for the nonexploitation of two-thirds of the string types resulting from the application of Rule 2, it is worth explaining the conditions favoring the exploitation of the remaining nine string types. First, it seems reasonable to assume that one might most readily imagine the necessarily animate derivatives of the categories D ($M_1 + M_1'$) and LA ($M_2 + M_2'$) as agents. This assumption is borne out by the fact that all but one of the exploited strings generated by Rule 2 figure among the first 18. String 19 stands as a unique exception, and we believe this exception can be accounted for in terms of a psychological "obscuring process" similar to that of *Verneinung*. In fact, string 19 represents a total reversal that provides the key to its nature. None of the other strings in which derivatives of the category DO appear as agents is ever exploited. Moreover, Plot types of the kind represented by string 19 are extremely rare. Perhaps only one important example exists: Euripides' *Medea.* In this play, it is the female character derivable from the actantial category DO that kills her brother (LA), kills her children by Jason (D), and banishes herself (DO). All of the eight remaining exploited Plot Types involve the destruction of the derivatives of the categories D and LA by derivatives of these same two categories. These eight remaining Plot Types can be classified in terms of the agent-patient relations exhibited in them.

Of the exploited strings 1, 2, 6, 8, 10, 13, 15, and 17, only one string, 8, contains sentences all of which are characterized by the appearance of derivatives of the same categories on both sides of the symbol A. It represents a unique Plot Type. The only example of this Plot Type, in our corpus, is Sophocles' *Antigone.* According to Aristotle, plays like *Antigone* exhibit the worst kind of Plot. Aristotle's objection to this Plot Type can perhaps be explained in terms of the formal characteristics of the string type involved. The difficulty with the *Antigone* Plot Type lies in the fact that the "reflexiveness" of the initial transitive relation of tragic myth is too clearly paralleled in the "isomorphic" self-destructive acts detailed in string 8. In keeping a balance between the evocation and the repression of the individual's "suicidal" desire for nonexistence, the information-obscuring process of Plot generation just barely succeeds with Tragic Plots derived from string 8. Of course, from the point of view of the imagination, string 8-type Plots are quite probable. It is their directness that makes them quite uncommon.

As soon as even one of the sets of "suicidal" sentences is replaced by a set of "nonsuicidal" sentences, things become much easier. Strings 2, 6, and 15, all of which contain two "suicidal sets" and one "nonsuicidal set," are all exploited. From among this group, string 6 seems to be the most effective, for it is represented by several important examples: Sophocles' *Oedipus Rex;* Shakespeare's *Antony and Cleopatra;* one of the Tragic Plots of *Romeo and Juliet,*[7] and Racine's *Andromaque.* One reason for the superior effectiveness of the Plot Type based on string 6 over those based on strings 2 and 15 surely lies in the distribution of the categories whose derivatives appear in the "suicidal sets." In string 6, it is the categories D and DO whose derivatives appear in them, and they are precisely the two categories that one imagines to be the most "cooperative" with the accomplishment of the desirer's end. Where the derivatives of the category LA appear in the sentences of "suicidal sets," imaginative difficulties arise.

Although Plot Types based on strings 2 and 15 exist, they are quite rare. String 15 is represented only by Euripides' *Hippolytus* and its descendants, e.g. Racine's *Phèdre*. We shall discuss this case in detail in a later chapter. For the moment, it may be suggested that the rarity of this Plot Type stems, in part at least, from the necessity of *Verneinung* or denial elements in plays utilizing it. (See the discussion of string 10 below.)

As the last remaining member of the group, string 2 constitutes a Plot Type intermediate in effectiveness and rarity between those based on strings 6 and 15. In our corpus, it is represented by Racine's *Mithridate* and one of the Tragic Plots of Shakespeare's *Othello*. Although it is not particularly well represented, the two examples we have of this Plot Type do provide an excellent appreciation of the imaginative necessities that go along with its utilization. It would seem that the utilization of string 2 in the generation of Tragic Plots requires the extreme magnification in importance of the central derivatives of either of the categories D (M_1) or LA (M_2) at the expense of the other. Thus, in *Mithridate,* the chief derivative of the category LA, Mithridate himself, is given central importance, whereas the chief derivative of the category D, Pompey, is relegated to allusions to events occurring before those of the play and "represented" in the play only by his functional partner Pharnace. In *Othello,* on the other hand, in the Tragic Plot concerned with Othello's marrying Desdemona against her father's will — the less interesting plot to be sure — the chief derivative of the category D, Othello, is given extreme importance over Brabantio, who occupies only a very small place of interest in the play. Extreme emphases on one aspect or another in a play usually have far-reaching parallels in many of the imaginative domains of the work. This point is particularly clear in cases involving *Verneinung* or denial. (See chapter 5.)

Of the three exploited Plot Types (1, 10, and 17) based on strings containing only one "suicidal set" of Plot sentences, only one (10) involves extensive *Verneinung* processes. String 10 is represented only by one example, the "main" Tragic Plot of Shakespeare's *Othello*. As in Euripides' *Hippolytus* and Racine's *Phèdre,* the most pivotal piece of information in the play is the lie told about an "alleged desirer." We are told that Hippolytus does not "possess" Phaedra and that Cassio does not "possess" Desdemona, but because lies are told about both of these "potential desirers" having succeded in their alleged aims, the idea of these "possessions" is at work in the play. In the Plot Types represented by *Hippolytus* and *Othello,* the reversal processes of *Verneinung* are illustrated by the assignment of the predominant agent function to derivatives of the category LA, i.e., to those actants who least readily assume this function, instead of to the derivatives of the category D, i.e. those actants who most readily assume this function. Furthermore, from the point of view of Character, it is the derivatives of the category DO that are made to seem "desiring" in a reversal of the desired-desiring functions.

Finally, it is to be noted that *Verneinung* processes are quite effective in obscuring dangerous information, but their very effectiveness may make plays characterized by them almost too obscure to understand. Perhaps the rarity of examples of the Plot Types represented by *Hippolytus* and *Othello* can be accounted for on this basis. That is, such Plot Types are effective only in optimal cases, and these cases undoubtedly involve the carrying of the *Verneinung* processes so far that they cannot help but be perceived. Since the Plot Type represented by *Hippolytus* and *Phèdre* involves agents derived from both the categories DO and LA, it is less extreme, in a sense, than that represented by *Othello,* which involves agents derived from only one category, LA. Later discussion will show that the Hippolytus myth can easily fall out of the tragic sphere by slightly increasing the lack of extremeness of the *Verneinung* cues necessary for the understanding of its underlying Plot structure.

The direct opposite of the Plot Type based on string 10 (*Othello*) is that based on string 1. Here, all of the agents are derivatives of the category D. Since these derivatives are the ones that most readily assume the function of agent, this Plot Type is fairly well represented. Examples from our corpus include Sophocles' *Electra,* Shakespeare's *Julius Caesar,* and Racine's *Britannicus.* Of course, the "one-sided" agent situation represented in string 1 constitutes another "extreme" device, and, consequently, tragedies featuring it are not of the most common variety. In Plot Types based on string 17, by contrast, three different sets of agents are involved. However, the reintroduction of the derivatives of the category LA as agents renders this Plot Type no more common than the previous one. It is represented in our corpus by Sophocles' *The Women of Trachis;* one of the Tragic Plots of Shakespeare's *Hamlet*[8]; *King John;* and *Richard II.*

There remains only one exploited Plot Type to be discussed. It is apparently the most common and the most effective. Based on string 13 above, it features what would appear to be the best imaginable combination of categories. First, no "suicidal sets" are present in string 13. This fact gives the Plot Type based on that string a distinct advantage. Second, the burden of the agent function is placed predominantly on the derivatives of the category D (M_1 and M_1'). Third, these derivatives are agents with respect to the derivatives of just those categories to which they are opposed functionally (LA and DO). Finally, no *Verneinung* processes are required here undoubtedly because the lack of "suicidal sets" provides sufficient obscurity. String 13 is the basis for the typical "revenge tragedy." Examples from our corpus include: Shakespeare's *Coriolanus;* one of the Tragic Plots of *Hamlet*[9]; *King Lear; Macbeth; Richard III;* one of the Tragic Plots of *Romeo and Juliet*[10]; *Timon of Athens; Titus Andronicus;* and Racine's *Bajazet* and *La Thébaïde.*

The following list resumes the representation, in our corpus, of the 27 Plot types discussed above:

1) *Electra, Julius Caesar, Britannicus*
2) *Mithridate, Othello* (II)
3), 4), and 5) not exploited
6) *Oedipus Rex, Antony and Cleopatra, Romeo and Juliet* (1), *Andromaque*
7) not exploited
8) *Antigone*
9) not exploited
10) *Othello* (I)
11) and 12) not exploited
13) *Coriolanus, Hamlet* (I), *King Lear, Macbeth, Richard III, Romeo and Juliet* (II), *Timon of Athens, Titus Andronicus, Bajazet, La Thébaïde*
14) not exploited
15) (Euripides' *Hippolytus*), *Phèdre*
16) Not exploited
17) *The Women of Trachis, Hamlet* (II), *King John, Richard II*
18) Not exploited
19) (*Medea*)
20)−27) not exploited

At this point, there remain eight categories to be transformed into the surface units of existing tragedies, viz. A, M_1, M_2, F, M_1', M_2', F', and ISA. We shall begin with the category A which involves the destructive acts representing the mythical act of self-annihilation. In the transformation of all these categories, we shall be using lexical rules. Most of these rules will have options and be context-sensitive. Each of the options provided for by rules with options will be possible under certain conditions empirically determined from a study of the corpus. These rules will apply independently to each element in a string to which they can apply, in such a way that the full range of options remains open for the rewriting of these elements.

Rule 6

A

Annihilates → banishes, blinds, castrates, destroys, kills, etc. (except in
the environments):

M_2 A M_2'
Initial Possessor Annihilates Functional partner of Initial Posses-
or . . . ,

M_2' A M_2' . . . ,
Functional partner of Initial Possessor Annihilates Functional
partner of Initial Possessor . . . ,

M_1 A M_1' . . . ,
Illegal Obtainer Annihilates Functional partner of Illegal Obtainer . . . ,

M_2' A   F . . . ,
Functional partner of Initial Possessor Annihilates Object of desire and possession . . . ,

M_2' A   F . . . ,
Functional partner of Initial Possessor Annihilates Functional
partner of Object of desire and possession . . . ,

F   A   F' . . . ,
Object of desire and possession Annihilates Functional partner of
Object of desire and possession . . . ,

F'   A
Functional partner of Object of desire and possession Annihilates
F . . .)
Object of desire and possession . . .)/

O (except in the environments:

M_1' A M_1' . . . ,
Functional partner of Illegal Obtainer Annihilates Functional partner of Illegal obtainer . . . ,

M_2' A M_1 . . . ,
Functional partner of Initial Possessor Annihilates Illegal Obtainer . . . ,

M_2' A M_1' . . . ,
Functional partner of Initial Possessor Annihilates Functional
partner of Illegal Obtainer . . . ,

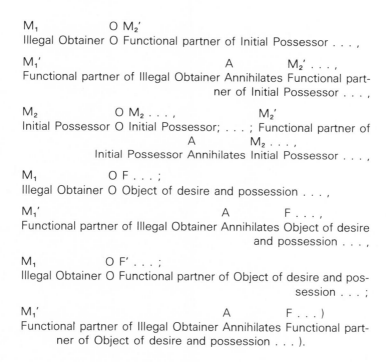

M₁   O M₂'
Illegal Obtainer O Functional partner of Initial Possessor . . . ,

M₁'   A   M₂' . . . ,
Functional partner of Illegal Obtainer Annihilates Functional part-
                                    ner of Initial Possessor . . . ,

M₂   O M₂ . . . ,   M₂'
Initial Possessor O Initial Possessor; . . . ; Functional partner of
                        A   M₂ . . . ,
            Initial Possessor Annihilates Initial Possessor . . . ,

M₁   O F . . . ;
Illegal Obtainer O Object of desire and possession . . . ,

M₁'   A   F . . . ,
Functional partner of Illegal Obtainer Annihilates Object of desire
                                    and possession . . . ,

M₁   O F' . . . ;
Illegal Obtainer O Functional partner of Object of desire and pos-
                                    session . . . ;

M₁'   A   F . . .)
Functional partner of Illegal Obtainer Annihilates Functional part-
        ner of Object of desire and possession . . .).

Rule 6 details the specific acts which can constitute imaginative representations of the abstract act of self-annihilation. It also
provides for the "voiding" of certain "unimaginable" strings or
parts of strings. Of course, the list of "destruction" verbs given
above is far from complete, but the completion of this list is
merely a matter of enlarging the corpus on which it is based.

What is interesting here are the conditions under which destructive acts may or may not be imagined. First, it seems unimaginable that one of the "central," i.e., nonprime, characters
performs a destructive act on one of his functional partners. M_1,
for example, cannot destroy M_1'. One reason is that it is the
central characters who are made to possess the socially desirable qualities that the tragic thinker wishes to present as ideals.
They, at least, can never participate actively in "disloyal" acts.
Second, the derivatives of the category M_2' will never destroy

themselves or any of the derivatives of the category DO. Here, the extremely one-sided nature of the characters derived from the category M_2', as derivatives of the category LA, becomes clear. These characters, unlike any derivative of M_2', are non-complex. They are oriented only to serving the overall purposes of the category LA. That is, they protect, but never destroy the derivatives of the category DO, and they destroy mainly the derivatives of the category D, from whom they must protect those of the category DO. They are seen as too uncooperative to destroy themselves and will only destroy their functional partner M_2 when the derivative of this category does not destroy himself. Third, the fact that the derivatives of the category M_2' are especially oriented towards the destruction of the derivatives of the category D is reflected in the necessity of rewriting the symbol A as a "verb of destruction" when it is preceded by M_2' and followed by a derivative of the category D (M_1 or M_1'). Finally, by contrast with the derivatives of the category M_2', the derivatives of the category M_1' are seen to be the most cooperative. For example, they must bring about their own destruction, where no other character will do so. (In fact, most of the conditions under which the symbol A may not be rewritten as "O" are designed to insure the destruction of those characters whose destruction is not necessarily accomplished by any one other character. Thus, for example, if the derivative of the category M_2 does not destroy himself, one or more of the derivatives of the category M_2' will have to destroy him.)

A considerable number of Plot sentences in the twelve-sentence strings resulting from the application of Rule 5 are voided because an unimaginable act must be rewritten as "O." This voiding of Plot sentences is one of the chief means by which Tragic Plots, most of which contain less than twelve Plot sentences, are obtained. Rules 10–12 will provide for even more possibilities for voiding Plot sentences. Preceding Rules 10–12 are three lexical rules without options.

Rule 7

M₁

Illegal Obtainer → Illegal Obtainer of F (Object of desire and possession), in extant tragedies, always a male character

Rule 8

M₂

Initial Possessor → Initial Possessor of F (Object of desire and possession), in extant tragedies, always a male character.

Rule 9

F

Object of desire and possession → Central Object of desire and possession, in extant tragedies, always a female character, a political
state, or some other piece of property, "governed" or "protected" by M₂

Rules 7 thru 9 terminate the derivation of the categories M_1, M_2,
and F. Proper names may be attached to the outputs of these
rules in such a way that M_1, M_2, and F are always represented
by one and the same character (actor) or object, as the case may
be, wherever these symbols appear in a string. The three
entities representing the categories M_1, M_2, and F form what we
shall call the "Central Desire Triangle" of any given Tragic Plot.

It is in the "Central Desire Triangles" of tragedies that the various "concrete" desire situations that can represent the individual beholder's "abstract" situation as a desirer are manifested.
As we have said in our discussion of tragic thought, the gratification of the individual's abstract desire to end his desiring
must be represented by the gratification of some particularly important, though "partial," concete desire. The symbols M_1, M_2,
and F can be rewritten in many different ways; in other words,
many "partial" desires may be important enough to represent
concretely an abstract desire for nonexistence. This thesis con-
tradicts the Freudian position that any derivatives of the
categories M_1, M_2, and F constitute "symbols" for the child, the
father (or *le nom du Père*[11]), and the mother, respectively. It is

true that, in tragedies like *Oedipus Rex*, the categories M_1, M_2, and F are represented by a configuration of characters including a child and his two parents. However, it is equally true that, in tragedies like *Othello,* these categories are represented by a configuration of characters including a suitor, a girl, and a father, or a lover, a wife, and a husband; and, in tragedies like *Macbeth,* these categories are represented by a configuration of entities including a subject, a king, and a country, and so forth. Precisely because the "Oedipal situation" occurs in some tragedies without having to be symbolized, we must consider it a situation parallel to many others which is not symbolized by them.

Of course, we do not discount the evidence on which the Freudian position is based; it is probable that infantile sexual desires are evoked in all tragedies. However, the evocation of these desires results from a conditioned association of any situation perceived by the adult as tragic with the first tragic situation he encountered as an infant. Because the first important forbidden object of desire the infant encounters is undoubtedly the mother; it is through this object and the legal authority preventing its possession that the individual usually "learns" the tragic sense of existence, i.e., desiring without hope of gratification. It is understandable, therefore, that, when the individual encounters other important forbidden objects of desire, he is reminded, in a sense, of his first tragic experience within the social microcosm of his family.

On the other hand, there is no reason to assume that all tragic situations must be understood in terms of the infant's relations with his parents. On the contrary, these situations correspond to a psychologically abstract configuration of elements according to which the individual is innately predisposed to conceive his relations to the external world of desired objects, and the first situation that corresponds to this model just happens to be the so-called Oedipal situation. Finally, the commonness of "family situations" in existing tragedies can best be accounted for on the basis of the universality of family experience. However, the existence of ostensibly "non-family" tragedies cannot be ignored. It is simply more theoretically adequate to define the tragic situation, not as the so-called Oedipal situation, but, rather, as the situation of the desiring individual whose one all-encompassing desire is no longer to desire at all.[12]

Rules 10–12 are lexical rules with options. They provide for the transformation of the categories M_1', M_2', and F' into characters (actors). As in the case of Rules 7–9, proper names may be attached to the derivatives of these symbols. However, one or more proper names may correspond to the same symbol since the same or a different name may be attached to each derivative of a symbol in a string.

Rule 10

M_1'

Functional partner of Illegal Obtainer → close male relative, heir, friend, ally, servant, etc. of Illegal Obtainer of Central Object of desire and possession (in extant tragedies, always a male character)/

O (except in the environments:

Illegal Obtainer of Central Object of desire and possession O M_2' [Functional partner of Initial Possessor of Central Object of desire and possession] . . . ; M_1' [Functional partner of Illegal Obtainer of Central Object of desire and possession/kills, etc.] but not O/M_2' [Functional partner of Initial Possessor of Central Object of desire and possession] . . . ,

Illegal Obtainer of Central Object of desire and possession O Central Object of desire and possession . . . ; M_1' [Functional partner of Illegal Obtainer of Central Object of desire and possession] kills, etc. Central Object of desire and possession . . . ,

Illegal Obtainer of Central Object of desire and possession O F' [Functional partner of Central Object of desire and possession] . . . ; M_1' [Functional partner of Illegal Obtainer of Central Object of desire and possession] . . .)

Rule 11

M_2'

Functional partner of Initial Possessor of Central Object of desire and possession → close male relative, heir, friend, ally, servant, etc. of Initial Possessor of Central Object of desire and possession /

O (except in the environments:

>Illegal Obtainer of Central Object of desire and possession kills, etc./O M_2' (Functional partner of Initial Possessor of Central Object of desire and possession) . . . ; any derivative of M_1' kills, etc./O M_2' (Functional partner of Initial Possessor of Central Object of desire and possession) . . . ,

Initial Possessor of Central Object of desire and possession O Initial Possessor of Central Object of desire and possession . . . ; M_2' (Functional partner of Central Object of desire and possession) kills, etc. (but not O) Initial Possessor of Central Object of desire and possession . . .)

Rule 12

F'

Functional partner of Central Object of desire and possession → close female relative, mother, wife, daughter, daughter-in-law, female friend, female servant, etc. of Illegal Obtainer of Central Object of desire and possession, Initial Possessor of Central Object of desire and possession, or Central Object of desire and possession /

O (except in the environments:

>Central Object of desire and possession O . . . ; F' (Functional partner of Central Object of desire and possession) kills, etc. (but not O) . . . , where " . . ." does not stand for a "prime" symbol or derivative of a "prime" symbol)

As in the case of Rule 6, the conditions placed on the options provided by Rules 10 through 12 assure the destruction of at least the central derivative from each of the categories D, LA, and DO. It is axiomatic that all three central derivatives must be destroyed in some way in every existing or possible tragedy. Upon the application of Rules 10 through 12, all of the characters of the Tragic Plot are obtained and their relationships established. It will be obvious, from an examination of the possibilities provided by these rules, that certain relationships or acts seem less than *vraisemblable*. For example, the rules provide for the possibility of a servant's banishing a king or a male character's castrating a female character. These acts must be voided by special minor rules which we shall call "selectional rules." Lying half in the domain of Tragic Plot generation and half in that of Diction, these rules simply provide for the verisimilitude of the surface information given in a work. We shall not attempt to present such rules, since they are not of far-reaching significance in the generation of Tragic Plots. There remains, then, one important and interesting rule to be presented, the rule which provides for the transformation of the category ISA into the concrete instruments of self-annihilation represented in existing tragedies.

Rule 13

ISA → sword/knife/dagger/poison/serpent/*grief*/ *madness*/etc.

Undoubtedly the most interesting thing about the list of possibilities provided by Rule 13 is that all of the items it contains except the two that are italicized belong to the class of so-called phallic symbols. We maintain, however, that these items are not phallic symbols; rather, they, as well as the phallus, are possible symbols for the abstract notion of a "tragic weapon." They, like the nonsexual tragic situations in which they figure, are but parallels of sexual phenomena. The occurrence of "grief" and "madness" in the same functional position in tragedies as other more apparent weapons of sudden destruction supports this claim. That grief and madness are imaginatively conceived as weapons of sudden, as opposed to chronic, destruction is illustrated in such linguistic expressions as "grief-stricken" and *frappé de folie*. Psychoanalysis, too, recognizes their function as instruments in its conception of the "sadism" of the superego on the ego.[13] In fact, the inadequacy of the Freudian position on the tragic is perhaps best revealed by its failure to integrate the conception of an internal "death struggle" with its conception of desire as ultimately sexual. In any case, it is to be noted that grief and madness as weapons are always used suicidally by some character on himself. Selectional rules should provide for this situation. Again, selectional rules will be necessary for establishing verisimilitude with regard to specific acts done with specific instruments.

To repeat what we said at the beginning of this chapter and of this section, the rules and grammar are presented above in their most primitive form. They are meant as a framework for adequately describing the structure of Tragic Plots. In some cases, the rules might have been presented more elegantly than they were here. However, the purpose of this introduction to the grammar of tragic myth has been to present its output and practical qualities in a way that might be immediately appreciable. Application of the rules to detailing the derivations of the two Tragic coplots of an existing tragedy, Shakespeare's *Romeo and Juliet*, should help to illustrate the functioning of the grammar of tragic myth.

3,vi. Tragic Plots, Coplots, and Subplots

The example of *Romeo and Juliet* illustrates many of the points made above and some others which must be made for the sake of descriptive adequacy. The play contains two Tragic coplots. We posit that, where a complete Tragic Plot exists in a work, other Tragic Plots contained in that work may be slightly agrammatical, i.e., lack certain elements provided for by the rules of the grammar of tragic myth. To what extent these "subplots" may be agrammatical is as yet undetermined. Where two complete Tragic Plots appear in the same work, we shall call them "coplots." However, the generation of each of them is rarely unaffected by the presence of the other. The presence of two coplots in *Romeo and Juliet* allows for the application of a minor but interesting rule of the grammar of tragic myth which has not yet been presented. Every tragedy must include the destruction of all of the three central derivatives of the categories D, LA, and DO. Where two or more Tragic Plots exist in the same tragedy and where the derivatives of the category M_2' are destroyed in both of them, it is not necessary that the derivatives of the category M_2 also be destroyed by a violent act. Instead, it seems sufficient that their destruction be imagined in terms of their being left without heirs. Finally, the generation of the Tragic Plots of *Romeo and Juliet* illustrates such phenomena as the voiding of unessential Plot sentences, the use of grief as an instrument of self-annihilation, and the role of the functional partners of the central derivatives of major categories. We shall begin with the generation of the "main" Tragic Plot of *Romeo and Juliet*, the personal tragedy of the lovers.

Romeo and Juliet I

The generation of the "main" Tragic Plot of *Romeo and Juliet* begins with the string: MSA A MSA ISA, the initial string in the derivations of all Tragic Plots. Applying Rule 1 to this string gives the string:

H A D ISA; H A LA ISA; H A DO ISA.

This string is also present in the derivations of all Tragic Plots. However, Rule 2 offers options, and, to generate the "main" Tragic Plot of *Romeo and Juliet*, we must choose option 6. Thus, we obtain the string:

M_1 A D ISA: M_1' A D ISA; H A LA ISA; H A DO ISA.

then the string:

M_1 A D ISA: M_1' A D ISA: M_1 A LA ISA; M_1' A LA ISA; H A DO ISA.

and, finally, the string:

M_1 A D ISA; M_1' A D ISA; M_1 A LA ISA; M_1' A LA ISA; F A DO ISA; F' A DO ISA.

Applying Rule 3, gives the string:

M_1 A M_1 ISA; M_1' A M_1 ISA; M_1 A M_1' ISA; M_1' A M_1' ISA; M_1 A LA ISA; M_1' A LA ISA; F A DO ISA; F' A DO ISA.

From Rule 4, we obtain the string:

M_1 A M_1 ISA; M_1' A M_1 ISA; M_1 A M_1' ISA; M_1' A M_1' ISA; M_1 A M_2 ISA; M_1' A M_2 ISA; M_1 A M_2' ISA; M_1' A M_2' ISA; F A DO ISA; F' A DO ISA.

Rule 5 gives the string:

M_1 A M_1 ISA; M_1' A M_1 ISA; M_1 A M_1' ISA; M_1' A M_1' ISA; M_1 A M_2 ISA; M_1' A M_2 ISA; M_1 A M_2' ISA; M_1' A M_2' ISA; F A F ISA; F' A F ISA; F A F' ISA; F A F' ISA.

At this point, the "attitudes" of each character are established with respect to himself and to the other characters of the Tragic Plot. It is clear that not all of the twelve actions reported by the twelve Plot sentences in the last string will be realized in the play. On applying Rule 6, some of the symbols "A" will be rewritten as "O"; others will be rewritten as "verbs of destruction." In certain cases, the rewriting of these symbols is determined by the conditions placed on the options available. However, in the cases where no conditions apply, sometimes one option will be exploited and sometimes another. From the applications of Rule 6, we obtain the string:

M_1 kills M_1 ISA; M_1' O M_1 ISA; M_1 O M_1' ISA; M_1' kills M_1' ISA; M_1 O M_2 ISA; M_1' O M_2 ISA; M_1 kills M_2' ISA; M_1' O M_2' ISA; F kills F ISA; F' O F ISA; F O F' ISA; F' destroys F' ISA.

Rules 7–9 give us the first proper names in the "main" Tragic Plot of *Romeo and Juliet*. From the application of Rule 7, we obtain the string:

Illegal Obtainer of Central Object of desire and possession = Romeo kills Illegal Obtainer of Central Object of desire and possession = Romeo ISA;

M_1' O Illegal Obtainer of Central Object of desire and possession = Romeo ISA;

Illegal Obtainer of Central Object of desire and possession = Romeo O M_1' ISA;

M_1' kills M_1' ISA; Illegal Obtainer of Central Object of desire and possession = Romeo O M_2 ISA;

Illegal Obtainer of Central Object of desire and possession = Romeo kills M_2' ISA; M_1' O M_2' ISA; F kills F ISA; F' O F ISA; F O F' ISA; F' destroys F' ISA.

Rule 8 gives the string:

Illegal Obtainer of Central Object of desire and possession = Romeo kills Illegal Obtainer of Central Object of desire and possession = Romeo ISA;

M_1' O Illegal Obtainer of Central Object of desire and possession = Romeo ISA;

Illegal Obtainer of Central Object of desire and possession = Romeo O M_1' ISA;

M_1' kills M_1' ISA; Illegal Obtainer of Central Object of desire and possession = Romeo O Initial Possessor of Central Object of desire and possession = Capulet ISA;

M_1' O Initial Possessor of Central Object of desire and possession = Capulet ISA;

Illegal Obtainer of Central Object of desire and possession = Romeo kills M_2' ISA; M_1' O M_2' ISA;

F kills F ISA; F' O F ISA; F O F' ISA; F' destroys F' ISA.

Rule 9 gives the string:

Illegal Obtainer of Central Object of desire and possession = Romeo kills Illegal Obtainer of Central Object of desire and possession = Romeo ISA; M_1' O Illegal Obtainer of Central Object of desire and possession = Romeo ISA;
Illegal Obtainer of Central Object of desire and possession=Romeo O M_1' ISA; M_1' kills M_1' ISA;
Illegal Obtainer of Central Object of desire and possession=Romeo O Initial Possessor of Central Object of desire and possession=Capulet

ISA; M_1' O Initial Possessor of Central Object of desire and possession=Capulet ISA;
Illegal Obtainer of Central Object of desire and possession=Romeo kills M_2' ISA; Central Object of desire and possession=
Juliet kills Central Object of desire and possession = Juliet ISA;
F' O Central Object of desire and possession = Juliet ISA;
Central Object of desire and possession = Juliet O F' ISA; F' destroys F' ISA.

Thus, the Central Desire Triangle of the "main" Tragic Plot is constituted by the suitor, Romeo; the daughter, Juliet; and the "enemy" father, Capulet. On considering the last string, we know that Romeo and Juliet will commit suicide and that Romeo will destroy some functional partner of Capulet, since no violent act is done on Capulet himself. Here, the Central Object of desire and possession, the chief derivative DO, is seen to be cooperative with the Desirer.

Rules 10–12 provide the full list of proper names involved in the destructive acts of the Tragic Plot, both as agents and as patients. From the application of Rules 10–12, we obtain the string:

Romeo kills Romeo ISA; O O Romeo ISA; Romeo O O ISA; O kills O ISA; Romeo O Capulet ISA; O O Capulet ISA; Romeo kills nephew of Capulet = Tybalt ISA; Friend of Romeo=Mercutio O nephew of Capulet = Tybalt ISA; Juliet kills Juliet ISA; O O Juliet ISA; Juliet O O ISA; Mother of Romeo=Lady Montague destroys Mother of Romeo=Lady Montague ISA.

Finally, the application of Rule 13 gives the specific instruments of self-annihilation used in the destructive acts of the play. Rule 13 gives the string:

Romeo kills Romeo with poison; O O Romeo with a knife; Romeo O O with a sword; O kills O with a knife; Romeo O Capulet with a dagger; O O Capulet with poison; Romeo kills Tybalt with a sword; Mercutio O Tybalt with a sword; Juliet kills Juliet with a dagger; O O Juliet with poison; Juliet O O with a knife; Lady Montague destroys Lady Montague with grief.[14]

At this point, a complete Tragic Plot has been generated. It contains the following surface information: Romeo kills himself with poison. Romeo kills Tybalt with a sword. Juliet kills herself with a dagger. Lady Montague destroys herself with grief, i.e., dies of sorrow. Nobody kills Capulet. Since Capulet represents one of the central figures in the Central Desire Triangle of the Tragic Plot, some further information must be given in order for the Plot to seem complete. It must be indicated that Capulet is left without an heir. In fact, throughout the play, the text reminds us that Juliet represents the only surviving child of Capulet. With her, the last of Capulet's heirs dies. At one point, he even says: "Death is my heir." In other words, Capulet is effectively destroyed because his lineage is destroyed. The ending of a bloodline as an imaginative equivalent to violently destroying a derivative of the category M_2 may have to be reinforced by the presence of a subplot or coplot in any given play. This possibility may be difficult to establish, since the number of plays in which the derivatives of the category M_2 are not violently destroyed is apparently very small. In any case, *Romeo and Juliet* does manifest a second Tragic Plot, the political tragedy, or what might be called the tragedy of the generations. It will be noted that the two Tragic Plots contained in the play are of different types. Whether or not any combinations of types of Tragic Plots can occur in one play is a matter for future investigation.

Romeo and Juliet II

Since the first steps in all derivations of Tragic Plots are always the same, we may begin the derivation of the second Tragic Plot of *Romeo and Juliet* with one of the strings resulting from the application of Rule 2. In this case, string 13, from the list of 27 basic options is exploited. The application of Rule 2 yields the string:

M_2 A D ISA; M_2' A D ISA; M_1 A LA ISA; M_1' A LA ISA; M_1 A DO ISA; M_1' A DO ISA.

When the categories D, LA, and DO are expanded by the application of Rules 3 thru 5, we obtain the string:

M_2 A M_1, ISA; M_2' A M_1, ISA; M_2 A M_1' ISA; M_2' A M_1' ISA; M_1 A M_2 ISA; M_1' A M_2 ISA; M_1 A M_2' ISA; M_1' A M_2' ISA; M_1 A F ISA; M_1 A F' ISA; M_1' A F ISA; M_1' A F' ISA.

Rule 6 provides the specific acts that take place in the Tragic Plot. From the application of this rule, we obtain the string:

M_2 banishes M_1, ISA; M_2' kills M_1, ISA; M_2 O M_1' ISA; M_2' kills M_1' ISA; M_1 O M_2 ISA; M_1' O M_2 ISA; M_1 kills M_2' ISA; M_1' kills M_2' ISA; M_1 disturbs F ISA; M_1' disturbs F ISA; M_1 O F' ISA; M_1' O F' ISA.

Rules 7–12 provide the proper names of the Tragic Plot. Their application yields the string:

Escales banishes Romeo ISA; Romeo kills Romeo ISA; Escales O O ISA; Romeo kills Tybalt ISA; Romeo O Escales ISA; O O Escales ISA; Romeo kills Paris ISA; Tybalt kills Mercutio ISA; Romeo disturbs (the peace and order of the state of) Verona ISA; Tybalt disturbs (the peace and order of the state of) Verona ISA; Romeo O O ISA; O O O ISA;

Finally, the application of Rule 13 provides the specific instruments of self-annihilation used in the Tragic Plot; it yields the string:

Escales banishes Romeo with his royal edict; Romeo kills Romeo with poison; Escales O O with a sword; Romeo kills Tybalt with a sword; Romeo O Escales with a dagger; O O Escales with poison; Romeo kills Paris with a sword; Tybalt kills Mercutio with a sword; Romeo disturbs the peace of Verona with a sword; Tybalt disturbs the peace of Verona with a sword; Romeo O O with a sword; O O O with poison.[15]

In the second Tragic Plot of *Romeo and Juliet,* as in the first, the derivative of the category M_2 is not violently destroyed. In the destruction of the "flower" of Verona's young nobility, it might be imagined that the Prince, like the older nobility, represented by Montague and Capulet, is left without heirs. However, the presence of coplots or subplots may simply allow for slight agrammaticalities. In any case, the most interesting feature of the "political" Tragic Plot of *Romeo and Juliet* is that Romeo appears as a derivative of both the categories M_1 and M_2'.

Here, we have an excellent example of the process of "condensation." As a representative of the "younger generation," Romeo is the chief disturber of the status quo. As the one who tries to keep the peace between Mercutio and Tybalt and as a friend of Mercutio, a kinsman to the Prince, Romeo represents a functional partner of the central legal authority. Tybalt qualifies as a derivative of the category M_1', not only because he is Romeo's counterpart among the representatives of the "younger generation," but also because he is actually a relative of Romeo, his cousin, at the moment he kills Mercutio. Paris is, of course, of the Prince's blood, and his character is completely in accord with the established order. That is, he behaves entirely "according to the social rules." From this derivation, it should be obvious that the same act can figure in more than one Tragic Plot and that it may signify different things in different contexts. Romeo's killing himself, for example, may be seen as a suicide in the first Tragic Plot, and as a murder in the second. It is the overall configuration of acts and characters, with their special relationships, that conveys the information of the Tragic Plot. It is clear that no superficially meaningful Plot sentence can adequately be understood in a literal sense. In the following chapters, we shall attempt to show how the overall configuration of dramatic elements in plays resembling tragedies can be used to account for the non-tragicness of these plays, especially where other criteria fail.

3,vii. Generation versus Scansion

In order to expound the rules of the grammar of tragic myth, we have presented the derivations of Tragic Plots from the point of view of the artist who generates them. An initial "deep" sentence, containing the information conveyed by the Tragic Plot has been transformed into sets of "surface" sentences containing the same information. Although the artist has certain options in the generation of Tragic Plots, his choices are limited, and he must proceed in an orderly fashion to apply various rules, i.e., to imagine his information according to certain regular predispositions.

The spectator or beholder of a tragedy, on the other hand, has no unique starting point for recapitulating the derivation of a Tragic Plot. Given all the possible outputs of the grammar of tragic myth, the spectator must somehow match the surface information he perceives to one of them. In many cases, he will be able to match this information to more than one of them, and, in these cases, we may say that the surface information is ambiguous. Of course, where a spectator cannot match the surface information he perceives with any output of the grammar, he cannot understand the work as a tragedy.

The process by which the spectator goes about trying to match the surface information with an output of the grammar of tragic myth may be called "scansion." The spectator must "scan" the information given in the surface sentence of a play for certain "landmarks." At this point, we cannot be sure just what these landmarks are, but we shall suggest some possibilities in the following chapters. We shall maintain that it is the failure of the spectator to recognize certain important landmarks that prevents him from appreciating a given work as a tragedy. By way of a test, we shall take up the cases of two controversial plays that hang on the edge of tragedy and discuss their deviation from authentically tragic forms.

Chapter Four

The Central Desire Triangle
of Tragic Myth

4,i. Landmarks

The spectator has no predetermined starting point for understanding the intelligible but meaningless Plot sentences presented to him on the surface of a play. On the other hand, he
must be able to "recognize" certain of the significant elements
belonging to Plot sentences resulting from the application of the
rules of the grammar of tragic myth. Undoubtedly, the easiest
significant elements for the spectator to recognize are those belonging to the restricted lexical lists of characters, objects, and
actions that figure in Tragic Plots. He knows, for example, that
such "deadly things" as chronic diseases or such Plot actions as
teaching or mowing the lawn do not belong to Tragic Plots. As a
working hypothesis, we suggest that the spectator begins unraveling the derivations of Tragic Plots by identifying the entities
in the play which qualify as derivatives of a certain lexical class
and proceeds by "fitting" other elements to these initially recognized entities, somewhat in the manner of a jigsaw puzzle.

We suggest that the first entity the spectator looks for in
scanning the surface Plot sentences of a play is the derivative of
the category F. In other words, he searches for an object belonging to the class of objects whose possession is desirable enough
to represent the abstract notion of desiring itself. As we have
said, there is no unique object of this kind. However, the list is
quite restricted, since the number of "partial objects of desire"

more or less universally imagined as "almost total" must be very small. In any case, the presence of such an object in the derived surface Plot sentences of a play is just a potential landmark, for it might appear there without having any functional importance. It is the identification of a complete configuration including this entity and other entities qualifying as derivatives of the categories M_1 and M_2 that will permit the spectator to advance towards an understanding of the Tragic Plot. Of course, given the presence of what we have called the "Central Desire Triangle" in a Tragic Plot, the spectator can label the nature of the play's "conflict" in terms of the nature of the entity derived from the category F. Thus, the presence of a real conflict situation can serve as a landmark in the understanding of Tragic Plots, as does the presence of a Central Desire Triangle.

The notion of conflict in tragedy is a recent one. It is foreign to most of the traditional views of tragedy stemming from Aristotelian doctrine. Underlying the Aristotelian conception of an "error in judgment," is an implicit assumption that no genuine conflict situations really occur; "correct reasoning" can, theoretically, prevent disaster. The actions betraying an error in judgment are mistaken actions, not necessary and willed, leading to the gratification of a desire by "dissolving" the frustrating conflict in which that desire is conceived. In many tragedies, it is, in fact, impossible to identify real errors in judgment. Often, those actions that seem to be "mistakes" are the result of correct reasoning but insufficient knowledge; at other times, actions performed with sufficient knowledge that nevertheless lead to disaster may be "errors" but are not necessarily errors in judgment. In short, although one cannot always situate some error in a tragedy, one can always find a conflict in it; one can always find a source of dispute and sets of disputers.

Thus, the Central Desire Triangle of a Tragic Plot stands as a primary landmark, and the functional partners of the participants in this Central Desire Triangle can be filled in by deduction. Of course, not only the characters or entities constituting the Central Desire Triangle must be identified. The spectator must also identify actions that correspond to the lexical list of acts that can represent the act of self-annihilation. Finally, where all of the proper characters, entities, configurations, and actions have been identified, the spectator may proceed with his recapitulation of the derivation of a Tragic Plot, having fitted together all the elements of an output of the rules of the grammar of tragic myth.

The case of Shakespeare's *Troilus and Cressida* provides a good opportunity for illustrating the importance of establishing a Central Desire Triangle of "regular" or "qualified" entities and of identifying the actions in which these entities participate, either as agents or as patients, as genuinely tragic acts.

4,ii. *Troilus and Cressida*`

For the sake of argument, we shall assume that, from the point of view of the medium, *Troilus and Cressida* resembles most tragedies. That is, as a serious drama, *Troilus and Cressida* possesses the same diction and spectacle features as most undisputedly tragic works. From the point of view of character, there is little basis for distinguishing *Troilus and Cressida* from genuine tragedies. Among the "Homeric stars" featured in the play, there are many whose extraordinary qualities might make them ideal models for the central figures in a tragedy. Even Pandarus, whose role as a figure of comic relief is perhaps more extensive than that of any other Shakespearean tragic character, does not exceed in his comic effects the limits of serious drama. Although *Troilus and Cressida*'s status as a tragedy is highly controversial, we might expect at least the secondary aspects of the play to resemble those of tragedies. However, a consideration of the Story Line of the play will reveal the difference between it and any genuine tragedy.

It will be remembered that the Story Line information in a work of art consists of both those sentences that report states of affairs and those sentences that report Plot actions. In determining the "conflict" in a given Story Line, one must pay particular attention to the sentences that report states of affairs. That is, it is the unstable combination of two or more states of affairs that necessitates the actions leading to a more stable situation.

Briefly, the important states of affairs in tragic situations are indicated by the substantial relations of the central figures in the Central Desire Triangle of a Tragic Plot. In other words, information must be given to the effect that the "desirer" desires the "desired object," that the "desirer" obtains the "desired object," and that the "desired object" is (initially) possessed or controlled by some "legal authority."

In *Troilus and Cressida,* there are many potential desired objects, i.e., derivatives of the category F, and many potential desirers, i.e., derivatives of the category M_1. With regard to this second category, however, it is clear that the number of potential derivatives is reduced by the fact that not only must a character be a desirer to qualify as a derivative of the category M_1, he must also be an "obtainer." There are at least five possible desirer-desired object pairs to orient the spectator's attention in the play. They include: Achilles-Troy, Achilles-Briseis, Paris-Helen, Diomedes-Cressida, and Troilus-Cressida. If any of these pairs constitutes a part of a tragic Central Desire Triangle, then the spectator has at least a chance of perceiving a Tragic Plot in *Troilus and Cressida.*

From the outset, it is obvious that the story of Achilles and Briseis is of no interest whatsoever. Although we are told by the doxological tradition that Achilles desires Briseis, this state of affairs never gives rise to any significant Plot actions. Besides, the story is much too far from the mainstream of the play's preoccupations to attract the spectator's attention. The same may be said, if less emphatically, about the stories of Achilles against Troy, and of Paris and Helen. In fact, these stories undoubtedly constitute complete Tragic Plots and are the basis for the Greek epic-tragedy of the Trojan War. However, the interest of the spectator in Shakespeare's play is directed to basically amorous, and not political, conflicts. Of course, the two are present in the play, since *Troilus and Cressida* is built on two fairly independent Story Lines, but, as the case of Shakespeare's treatment of the story of Achilles and Patroclus will show, the sexual aspect of what might be conceived as a political tragedy is dominant. In any case, a consideration of the character's personal relationships, reveals the lack of genuine Central Desire Triangle in the play.

It is clear that Troilus desires Cressida, and these characters can represent derivatives of the categories M_1 and F, respectively. However, one is hard pressed to find a real representative of the category M_2 to fill out the necessary configuration. Of course, Calchas has some claim to Cressida, and he, along with the Greeks, may, perhaps, be conceived as derivatives of the category LA. In this case, however, neither Troilus nor any other character accomplishes the destruction of the derivative of the category M_2, nor even of its functional partners. Thus, the state of affairs involving Troilus' love for Cressida does not give rise to a Tragic Plot, for there is no real conflict situation to be resolved.

Since Troilus actually "possesses" Cressida at one point, he may also be imagined as a derivative of the category M_2. Here, Diomedes who replaces him qualifies as a derivative of the category M_1, where Cressida remains the derivative of the category F. Although this situation, like the preceding one, is central enough to orient the spectator's attention, no real conflict exists. No tragic acts are performed and the participants in the Central Desire Triangle are not destroyed. Again, it must be emphasized that it is the destruction of the configuration we have called the Central Desire Triangle, and not the death of the "hero," as A. C. Bradley might maintain, that is important for the tragicness of a play.[1]

Finally, the story of Achilles, Patroclus, and Hector provides an interesting example of a potential agrammaticality in a nearly Tragic Plot. Despite Plato's comments on the relationship between Achilles and Patroclus, Shakespeare insists on making Patroclus the "desired object" in the story. Achilles may be imagined as his "protector" and, consequently, as a derivative of the category M_2. Although Patroclus, as a male figure, does not qualify, as a derivative of the category F, we shall suppose, for the moment, that he can occupy the corresponding position in a tragic Central Desire Triangle. In this case, the derivatives of both the categories F and M_2 are destroyed in the general myth. If we suppose that Hector can qualify as a derivative of the category M_1, then the play might contain a complete Central Desire Triangle and the tragic actions necessary for its destruction. That is, the only real acts of destruction that can qualify as representatives of the act of self-annihilation occur in the story in question. Of course, the suppositions we have made require some support, and this support is hard to find. By some stretching of the imagination, we can perhaps conceive of Patroclus as an object of desire in which is "invested" Achilles' potential power as a "legal authority." In this case, it might even be possible to conceive of Hector as "desiring" to control Patroclus' fate. However, even after allowing for all of the imaginative leeway possible, the ultimate reason for the nontragicness of the story and, consequently, of the play can be identified as the impossibility of fitting a male character into the place grammatically occupied by a derivative of the category F in an output of the grammar of tragic myth. That is, regardless of the interpretative possibilities for construing various functions in the play, the grammar itself can provide an ultimate criterion for tragicness. Because it is descriptively adequate, the grammar can stand as a "control" on interpretative casuistry.

From another point of view, the grammar of tragic myth can help in explaining the closeness of certain works to tragedy. In the case of Shakespeare, for example, it can illustrate the points at which nearly tragic nontragic plays like *Troilus and Cressida* and *The Merchant of Venice* deviate from the tragic system. Both of these plays contain potential Central Desire Triangles, but, as we have shown in the case of *Troilus and Cressida,* either these configurations are somehow incomplete or anomalous or they give rise to no tragic acts. It is interesting to note that both plays contain the same anomaly, in a sense; that is, they feature homosexual "attitudes" in potentially tragic situations.[2] On this basis, it may be possible to show how the psychological performance model of one author, for example, may provide for various idiosyncratic restrictions on the imagination of tragic situations, or, conversely, how such a model might provide for the nonvoiding of certain paratragic configurations of elements until fairly late in the process of Plot generation.[3]

In short, the gain in explanatory adequacy accompanying the grammar of tragic myth that we have presented here over other theories of tragedy can be perceived in many ways. First and most important, it is evidenced in the superior descriptive adequacy of the grammar of tragic myth. However, this gain is also reflected in the possibilities the grammar provides for characterizing the nontragic in works related intuitively to tragedy. As we have shown, in the case of *Troilus and Cressida,* the nontragic may result from deviations from the tragic system, and these deviations may be identified and even classified formally by referring to the grammar of tragic myth. The frequency and consistency of use of deviant derivational operations in generating paratragic Plots by particular writers, schools, and periods should provide a large field of study, just as the frequency and consistency of use of grammatical derivational operations in the generation of genuine Tragic Plots. In the following chapter, we shall discuss some of the ways in which a Tragic Plot can be paralleled by tragic and nontragic variants. In so doing, we shall attempt to explain how some Tragic Plots can bear very little modification if they are to remain genuinely tragic.

Chapter Five

Tragic and Nontragic Variants

5, i. Differences in Plot and Differences in Purpose

A single story told in different ways often serves the aesthetic and intellectual purposes of both tragic and nontragic thinkers. It should be possible, on the basis of Plot structure variations, to show how one variant of a basic story lends itself to tragedy and how others lend themselves to other genres. In this chapter, we shall consider the Plot structures of Euripides' *Hippolytus* and Racine's *Phèdre,* as well as those of some nondramatic works resembling these plays. It will be maintained that *Hippolytus* is a genuine tragedy, whereas *Phèdre* is only a tragedy "by association." That is to say, *Phèdre* is only understood as a tragedy by those who are so strongly conditioned by their experience of Euripides' *Hippolytus* (and Seneca's *Phaedra*) that they "ignore" important pieces of information presented in Racine's play.[1] The popular success of *Phèdre* cannot be accounted for entirely on the basis of the play's effectiveness as a tragedy. It has served nontragic purposes. As a final hypothesis, it will be suggested that at least some of the purposes served by works related to tragedy are related to the purposes served by tragedies. Whether it is presented tragically or nontragically, the Hippolytus myth, for example, lends itself particularly well to the expounding of the practical value of observable character traits possessed by ideal figures. We shall attempt to explain this fact in terms of the psychological mechanisms involved in the variant generations of the basic story.

It was noted, in the general discussion of the 27 fundamental

Tragic Plot types resulting from the application of Rule 2 of the grammar of tragic myth, that the Tragic Plot type underlying *Hippolytus* and *Phèdre* is very rarely exploited in actual tragedies. The rarity of this Tragic Plot type (Type 15) can be accounted for in terms of a distribution of agent-patient functions that is apparently relatively difficult to imagine. In order to be effective, such a distribution must be reinforced with *Verneinung*-like devices, and the balancing of distributional and *Verneinung* elements is a delicate matter. We shall take the combination of elements embodied in Euripides' *Hippolytus* as optimal and attempt to illustrate how variants and cognates lose in effectiveness through deviation.

5,ii. Euripides' Hippolytus

The agent-patient relationships in the Tragic Plot of *Hippolytus* are detailed in the basic string:

M_2 A M_1 ISA; M_2' A M_1 ISA; M_2 A M_1' ISA; M_2' A M_1' ISA; M_2 A M_2 ISA; M_2' A M_2 ISA; M_2 A M_2' ISA; M_2' A M_2' ISA; F A F ISA; F' A F ISA; F A F' ISA; F' A F' ISA.

(This string corresponds to an output of Rule 5 of the grammar of tragic myth.) Thus, the agents of the Tragic Plot are the derivatives of the categories M_2, M_2', F, and F'. In earlier discussions, we noted that the derivatives of the categories M_1 and M_1' are most easily imagined as agents, whereas the derivatives of the categories M_2 and M_2' are least easily imagined as agents. Although not all of the agents in the Tragic Plot of *Hippolytus* are derivatives of the categories M_2 and M_2', their choice represents a fairly extreme reversal of the "expected" situation. It is the nontotality of this reversal that renders the Tragic Plot type in question here somewhat unstable. In any case, the reversal of agent roles in *Hippolytus* is paralleled by a large number of *Verneinung*-like reversals in the text. These exaggerated or extreme devices include: (1) Hippolytus' absolute chastity; (2) Phaedra's loving Hippolytus, instead of Hippolytus' loving

Phaedra; (3) Phaedra's attempt to keep her passion secret; (4) the Nurse's betrayal of Phaedra to Hippolytus and Phaedra's unwillingness to tell Hippolytus of her love herself; (5) the oath of secrecy Hippolytus gives to the Nurse and his refusal to justify himself to Theseus because of it; (6) Phaedra's posthumous lie concerning Hippolytus' attack on her; and others which are too unimportant to mention. All of these devices are simple and direct, and, in their extremeness, they compensate for the lack of total reversal on the level of Plot generation.

Because the Tragic Plot is based on reversal, it successfully embodies two ''suicidal'' actions: Phaedra's suicide and Theseus' self-destruction through grief. Although Theseus is neither dead nor left without heirs at the end of the play, we are convinced that he is effectively destroyed. Versions of the overall legend provide for Theseus' eventual self-banishment, and the text of the play is explicit. Theseus himself says:

Ὄλωλα, τέκνον, οὐδέ μοι χάρις βίου.
(I, too am dead now. I have no more joy in life.)

Theseus' destruction is necessary for the completion of the tragic design, and it is Racine's elimination of this element that accounts, at least in part, for the nontragicness of the actual text of his *Phèdre*.

5,iii. Phèdre

The basic string underlying the Tragic Plot of Phèdre is the same as that underlying the Tragic Plot of *Hippolytus*. However, the developments of some of the sentences in this string differ in the generation of the two Tragic Plots. In *Hippolytus*, all but three sentences are voided. Only the sentences:

M_2' A M_1 ISA; M_2 A M_2 ISA; F A F ISA;

are developed to yield the Plot actions:

Neptune destroys Hippolytus . . . ; Theseus destroys Theseus . . . ; Phaedra kills Phaedra . . . ;

In *Phèdre,* all but three sentences are voided, but only the sentences:

M_2' A M_1 ISA; F A F ISA; F' A F' ISA.

are developed to yield the following Plot actions:

Neptune destroys Hippolyte . . . ; Phèdre kills Phèdre; Oenone kills Oenone . . .

The most important thing to be noted here is that, in *Phèdre,* the derivative of the category M_2 is not destroyed. Theseus is not even left without heirs, and the closing lines of the play stress this detail:

Que, malgré les complots d'une injuste famille, Son amante aujourd'hui me tienne lieu de fille.

Because there is no destruction of the representatives of the legal authority, and especially of the representative of the category M_2, the play is not tragic. The nontragic "usefulness" of the play will be discussed presently.

For the moment, it is worthwhile noting the repercussions of eliminating the destruction of the derivative of the category M_2. This derivational choice represents a weakening of the reversal devices characteristic of the "Ur-myth," in that it involves the elimination of a most "unexpected" agent, M_2. Similarly, in *Phèdre*, all of the original reversal devices, except, of course, the desire of the female character for the male character, are in some way weakened. Hippolyte is neither completely chaste nor exaggeratedly misogynous. He is in love with Aricie and does not go into a long tirade against women when Phèdre reveals her love for him. Racine's Phèdre discloses her secret to her nurse somewhat more easily than Euripides' heroine, and it is she, rather than the nurse, who tells Hippolyte of her love. Consequently, when it comes time to justify himself, Hippolyte is not bound by an oath of secrecy. Instead, his silence is explained simply in terms of respect for his father. Finally, it is the nurse, rather than Phèdre, who accuses Hippolyte, and Phèdre's eventual confession nullifies the original lie completely. The lack of extremeness in these details makes for their ineffectiveness as reversal devices. On the other hand, this lack of extremeness concentrates attention on the ethical importance of superficial qualities.

5,iv. The Portrayal of Character Traits and their Practical Value

The presentation of characters with some good and some bad qualities permits the artist consciously and unconsciously to contrast the practical values of the spectator's identifying with these characters through these qualities. Partial reversal devices are particularly well suited to the conscious division of character traits along ethical lines. Because these devices are not always understood as negations of bits of "obscured" information, they must sometimes be understood in terms of "surface" information. Their artistic unintelligibility sets them off as centers of didactic interest. In *Phèdre,* for example, the Christian ideals with which the spectator is meant to identify are embodied in Hippolyte's humility and honor and in Phèdre's confession and repentance. The peculiarly Jansenist notion of predestination is expounded in three examples:

1) Although his character traits are unilaterally desirable, from a Christian point of view, Hippolyte is condemned to a miserable end.
2) Although Phèdre is basically evil, she repents and is worthy of pardon, yet she too is condemned to an unhappy end.
3) Thésée, who possesses basically non-Christian qualities (he lacks charity and mercy, for he is quick to condemn his own son to death), is "saved."

In short, there are no concrete character-proofs guaranteeing salvation or damnation. The practical value of possessing given qualities is, then, unclear with respect to the attainment of nonexistence. By contrast, in genuine tragedy, the practical value of possessing specific qualities must always be made clear precisely through an association of concrete character traits with personal destiny. Finally, Racine uses the occasion to create aesthetic identifications in a completely negative way. That is to say, he creates none at all. When *Phèdre* is not appreciated as a tragedy, by association with its literary antecedents, it is, then, apt to serve simply as a conscious demonstration of the unpredictibility of fate.

It sometimes happens that genuinely tragic works are as readily appreciated nontragically as they are tragically, especially when they contain disorienting elements. Partial reversal devices can be disorienting elements, in that the spectator is initially unsure whether he should understand the information conveyed by them superficially or through derivation. Based on the same situation as the Hippolytus myth, *La Chastelaine de Vergi,* a thirteenth-century French romance, provides an excellent example of a "partial reversal" Plot structure that lends itself to superficial, as well as to tragic, interpretation. The basic string underlying the Tragic Plot of *La Chastelaine de Vergi* is of the form:

M_1 A M_1 ISA; M_1' A M_1 ISA; M_1 A M_1' ISA; M_1' A M_1' ISA; M_2 A M_2 ISA; M_2' A M_2 ISA; M_2 A M_2' ISA; M_2' A M_2' ISA; M_2' A F ISA; M_2' A F ISA; M_2 A F' ISA; M_2' A F' ISA.

Three sentences from this string are developed to give the Plot actions:

The chevalier kills the chevalier . . . ; the duc banishes the duc . . . ; the duc kills the duchesse . . .;

Because the string underlying the Tragic Plot (string Type 7) contains sentences of the form: M_2 A F ISA; M_2' A F ISA; M_2 A F' ISA; M_2' A F' ISA; it is not exploited in dramatic tragedies. However, a complete Central Desire Triangle exists and is destroyed, and the work can therefore be appreciated tragically.

The Tragic Plot structure exhibits a certain amount of reversal, since the derivatives of the category LA assume two-thirds of the agent functions. On the other hand, there is less reversal than in *Hippolytus* or *Phèdre*, for M_1 and M_1' appear as agents in *La Chastelaine de Vergi*. By contrast with the devices in the dramatic works we have been discussing, the partial reversals in *La Chastelaine de Vergi*, represented by the young man's loving another woman and the breaking of oaths of secrecy by him, by the duc, and by the duchess, are, in some sense, "proportional" to the partial reversals on the level of Plot generation. Nonetheless, those partial reversals lend themselves to superficial interpretation, as well as understanding through derivation. The work ends in an explicit "moral":

> Et par cest example doit l'en
> s'amor celer par si grant sen
> c'on ait toz jors en remembrance
> que li descouvrirs riens n'avance
> et li celers en toz poins vaut.
> Qui si le fet, ne crient assaut
> des faux felons enquereors
> qui enquierent autrui amors.

In short, the concrete actions involved in the partial reversals become subjects for didactic interest, even though there is the alternative possibility of understanding them as manifestations of more abstract actions.

5,v. Situations versus Plots

In the context of a discussion on variants, one important point needs to be made. Similar situations or initial "states of affairs"[2] do not always give rise to Plots that can be considered variants. The fact that isolated elements or sets of elements resemble each other in different works does not imply that it is possible to demonstrate any systematic development, in these works, from a basic pattern. Based on the same underlying themes as *Phèdre* and *La Chastelaine de Vergi*, the *Lai de Lanval*, by Marie de France, for example, seems to bear little or no systematic resemblance to tragic or paratragic works. Since none of the

concrete Plot actions characterizing the tragic and paratragic variants of the story occurs in this work, there is no reason to assume that the process of Tragic Plot generation is ever actually
undertaken. To return to a hypothesis proposed earlier, the
feminine authorship of the work may account for the nontragic
treatment of the initial situation. In any case, the work's main
interest lies in its descriptions of wealth, beauty, and magic; it
does not seem particularly well-suited to expressing ethical
ideals.

In conclusion, the grammar of tragic myth is not designed to
be a basis for the critical analysis of all narrative works. First and
foremost, it is a conceptual framework for the consideration of
(dramatic) tragedies. It should be useful in dealing with nondramatic tragic works and with paratragic works of all sorts.
However, the grammar of tragic myth should not be particularly
useful in accounting for the effectiveness of works that serve
purposes unrelated to those of the tragic thinker. Finally, the
predictive power of the grammar in determining the member-
ship of works of art in a functional genre lies in the specification
of the grammar's object, as well as in the descriptive adequacy
of the grammar.

Conclusion

The chief purpose of this work has been to establish an adequate conceptual framework for the consideration of tragedy and the tragic. By way of reasonable speculation, a number of hypotheses have been proposed. These hypotheses are meant to throw light on the creation and appreciation of the tragic in tragedy and on the artistic production of tragic pleasure. We have maintained that the tragic in tragedy consists specifically of the expression of a certain kind of aesthetically useful information. In tragedy, as opposed to other manifestations of tragic thought, this information is "poetically obscured." That is, its form is such that it allows for the relatively painless evocation of (painful) desires. Consequently, its expression, in individual tragedies, takes on a multitude of apparently unrelated forms. The systematic establishment of the common genealogy of these forms is accomplished by means of a theoretical model describing the writer-spectator's imaginative possibilities for deriving them from a common source.

The tragic involves the representation of the destruction of what we have called a Central Desire Triangle, a tripartite microcosm of the social order as the individual conceives it. This representation consists of the expression of the information that a mythical self-annihilator (the social microcosm personified) annihilates, i.e., destroys, himself with an instrument of self-annihilation. In believing this information, the spectator is reassured that it is possible to escape from the desire-gratification cycle of existence. Through the heroic ideals presented to him, he learns that the attainment of nonexistence is difficult, but he can be content in the hope that he may ultimately achieve bliss. This contentment is tragic pleasure in all its intensity.

In tragedy, the information essential to the production of tragic pleasure is expressed through the aurally and visually perceptible medium of drama. Although it should be possible to describe the derivation of particular arrangements of significant dramatic elements from an abstract proposition embodying what we have called tragic myth, we have not attempted to do so. Instead, we have supposed that these arrangements can be semiotically standardized, i.e., intersemiotically translated into simple linguistic propositions. Consequently, we have attempted to describe the derivation of simple, though informationally complete, linguistic resumés of dramatic expressions. In order to describe formally the derivation of surface forms of tragic expression, we have developed a transformational generative grammar of Tragic Plots. Of course, it may be interesting to develop formal theories of tragic diction and spectacle, but these theories will only account for superficial resemblances among tragedies as serious dramas. For us, the essence of the tragic lies entirely within the Tragic Plot.

It must be remembered that the grammar of Tragic Plots presented here is an embryonic one. Although it claims to account for the basic structure of all tragedies, it leaves many large areas to be explored. For example, minor selectional rules governing the attribution of specific actions to specific subjects or specific objects to specific actions remain to be discovered. Apparently, particular characters (actors) can only accomplish imaginatively restricted sets of actions, and these actions can only be accomplished with regard to certain other characters or objects. Rules will be needed to account for possible combinations of Tragic Plot types in plays containing more than one Tragic Plot. Eventually, necessary balances among imaginative devices of all sorts may be discovered. The *Verneinung*-like processes of pretense, negation, and internal contradiction, for example, may formally parallel the other poetical obscuring devices of Plot generation, etc.

The grammar claims to generate an infinite number of Tragic Plots. In other words, it is not designed solely to describe a corpus of existing works. On the other hand, the grammar provides formal criteria for identifying and classifying actual tragedies. On the basis of particular features in the derivational histories of given Tragic Plots, tragedies may be grouped into psychologically and sociologically interesting classes. Resemblances among the works of one author, school, or tradition may be accounted for in a formal way. Finally, specific grammars, adequate for the description of particular classes of works, may eventually be developed.

With respect to theories of other genres, the theory of the tragic genre presented here should serve as a methodological forerunner. Nontragic works undoubtedly serve in producing special aesthetic effects. These special aesthetic effects may be based on the production of special states of belief, similar or analogous to the tragic belief in the possibility of attaining nonexistence. Because the production of states of belief involves the conveying of information, classes of works may be identifiable on the basis of bits of aesthetically useful information common to their members. In other words, nontragic genres, such as tragicomedy, farce, and various other types of comedy, may be describable by grammars designed to account for the expression of the basic information that notionally defines the genre. Since the rules of the grammar of tragic myth detail hypothetical universals in human imaginative processes, it might be expected that quite similar rules will appear in grammars of nontragic myth. In this context, it should be pointed out that grammars describing the artistic derivation of nonmythical, i.e., non-Plot information are also possible. For example, descriptive information about character or narrative-descriptive information about movement may be susceptible to the same sort of derivational obscuring processes as Plot information. Finally, the artistic adaptability of the grammar of tragic myth depends largely on the structural and teleological relations holding between tragedies and other works of art. The ethical and aesthetic purposes for using particular forms of expression must never be ignored.

By contrast, the psychological adaptability of the grammar depends mainly on the explanatory adequacy of the hypotheses underlying its development. The grammar of tragic myth is based on a hypothetical psychological performance model for describing certain human imaginative processes. To the extent that this model is adequate for tragedy, other models similar to it should be adequate for describing the psychological processes involved in the creation and use of such products of the human imagination as dreams, myths, and social institutions. For example, in the derivations of actual Tragic Plots presented above, we have illustrated how the universal psychological processes of decomposition and condensation can be formally described. In establishing an imaginative lexicon for tragedy and in introducing voiding conventions into the rules of the grammar, we have suggested ways in which imaginative symbolism may be limited. In short, the potential usefulness of rules like those of the grammar of tragic myth for formally describing psychological mechanisms is not to be underestimated.

In conclusion, we believe that the theory of the tragic genre presented here embodies many advances over previous theories of tragedy. First and most important, it provides an adequate formal description of the superficial structure of the tragic in actual tragedies. Second, because it details the various levels in the generation of the tragic, it permits the formulation of a great number of original theoretical generalizations. Third, it provides an adequate explanation for the aesthetic effectiveness of artistic expressions of tragic thought. Fourth, it provides a model for theorizing about certain nontragic and nonartistic phenomena. Fifth, it is simple and economical. Sixth, it uses generally accepted analytical devices not designed specifically to suit its own purposes. Last, but not least, it does not attempt to characterize as tragic irrelevant aspects of the dramatic vehicles for the expression of tragic thought that are its objects.

Appendix:
The Morphology
of Information in Art

A,i. Critical Categories

These appended remarks will involve little more than a set of formal definitions for some fundamental traditional critical notions. In formulating these definitions, we have attempted to establish parallels between the notions to be defined and certain grammatical notions. This procedure is meant to underline the a priori nature of the critical notions in question, and to serve as a deductive basis for a morphology of the information contained in all genuine works of art, and the status of "artistic information" as ordinary information in an aesthetic environment. Here, as elsewhere in this work, explicit definitions should be taken on their own merits, i.e., without reference to the usages of other theorists. Once these definitions are given, we shall attempt to demonstrate their peculiar usefulness, as we understand it, in relation to certain (superficially) similar theoretical undertakings.

A,ii. The Standardization of Informational Contents

Before the information contained in any given work of art can be studied by a method applicable to all art forms, i.e., music, literature, painting, etc., it must be "standardized." By standardizing the information contained in all works of art, we mean presenting it in a unique semiotic code, in this case a natural language, specifically English.[1] Other criteria for standardization, such as the reduction of redundancies,[2] may prove useful in certain critical situations. However, they are not necessary for a morphological analysis of informational contents and need not concern us here. What is important in the present context is that all that is intelligible in a work of art can and should be intersemiotically rendered into linguistic propositions.

The process of logical communication depends on the ultimate derivation, i.e., the understanding, of meaningful sentences. It is for this reason that standardized information will best be given in the form of propositions. For the purpose of uniformity and simplicity, we shall stipulate, furthermore, that all standardized propositions must be of a special type. These propositions should correspond roughly to the "kernel sentences" of early transformational grammar.[3] In other words, all standardized information will best be given in the form of simple, i.e., noncomplex and noncompound, declarative sentences, as they may be derived transformationally from other types of sentences present in an initial intersemiotic translation of the information contained in a given work of art. Finally, it should become clear that the morphology of standardized propositions, and, consequently, that of standardized informational contents, in general, should somehow recapitulate the derivation of the "phrase structure" of basic sentences.[4] Thus, we shall proceed with an analysis of basic propositional structure and, with the elucidation of each new grammatical category, we shall attempt to discover correspondences with interesting critical categories.

A,iii. Subjects and Predicates

In this section and in the sections that follow, we shall discuss the kinds of information conveyed by specific propositional formants on the basis of the sample sentences given below:

1) The house was old.
2) The trip seems too long.

3) The horse is running away.
4) John drives fast.
5) The man hit the dog with a stick.
6) Peter opens the door with a key.
7) Mary loves John passionately.
8) Love conquers all.

The largest, most fundamental, propositional formants are, of course, subjects and predicates, as we shall examine these logical categories first. Traditionally, logical subjects have been characterized as that about which something is predicated, and logical predicates have been characterized as that which is predicated (said) of a logical subject. In other words, the relation of logical subjects to logical predicates is a functional relation of mutual complementarity. The things about which something is predicated in sentences 1–8 are readily identifiable; they are, respectively, "the house," "the trip," "the horse," "John," "the man," "Peter," "Mary," and "love." In Hockett's terminology,[5] these logical subjects are referred to as "topics," while the things which are predicated of them are referred to as "comments." We reserve the term "topics," which belongs more particularly to the discipline of rhetoric than to that of grammar, for use in a different context.

Depending on the meaning of the term, we may say that sentences are "about" two different things at the same time. They are predications about subjects, and they are reports about events or states. Thus, no work of art, for example, is exclusively "about" its subject matter, i.e., the totality of logical subjects expressed in it. On the contrary, it is "about" this subject matter and "about" other things which we shall call its "themes." Themes involve states and events and constitute the "essential" part of propositional information in works of art. By "essential," we mean the opposite of "circumstantial"; we shall attempt to make this distinction clear by diagramming the fundamental logical categories of sentential phrase structure:

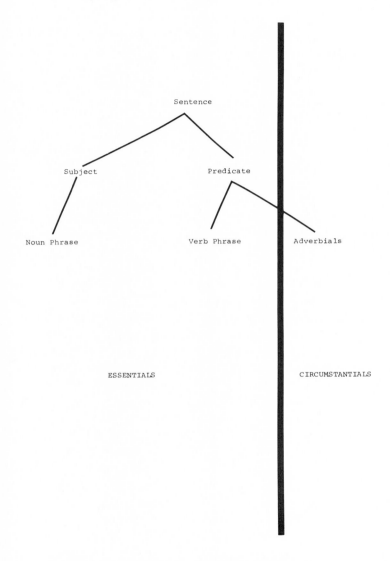

Of course, the identification of circumstantials with adverbials indicated in the phrase structure diagram above is commonplace in grammatical theory. On the other hand, the dialectically complementary nature of the remainder of the sentence as its essentials is usually ignored by grammatical theorists. In any case, we wish to emphasize that, where works of art are concerned, themes can be defined as the noncircumstantial elements in given informational contents. At this point, we can reintroduce the term "topic." We shall take topics to be identical with themes and define them, specifically, as the nominalized "labels" for the themes to which they correspond. In sentences 1−8 above, for instance, the essential, i.e., thematic, information is conveyed by the following expressions: 1) The house is . . . , 2) The trip seems . . . , 3) The horse is running away. 4) John drives . . . , 5) The man hit the dog . . . , 6) Peter opens the door . . . , 7) Mary loves John . . . , 8) Love conquers all. The topics of these sentences, however, represent the nominalizations of these expressions; they are, respectively: the being of the house, the seeming of the trip, the running away of the horse, John's driving, the man's hitting the dog, Peter's opening the door, Mary's loving John, and Love's conquering all. By distinguishing various thematic types, many important traditional notions can be formally defined. Before discussing these notions, however, we must say a few more words about the distinction between essentials and circumstantials in propositional information.

The term "essential" has a double implication. It suggests centrality and necessity. On the other hand, it also suggests a certain bareness and lack of detail. For this reason, we feel justified in claiming that all of the *descriptive* information in propositions and, consequently, in works of art, is provided by circumstantial expressions, i.e. by adverbials. With regard to the examples given above, it should be generally agreed that the descriptive elements in sentences 1−8 include the following expressions: "old," "too long," "fast," "passionately," "with a stick," and "with a key." The fact that this type of information is nonessential is illustrated by its absence from sentences 3 and 8. In any case, the distinction between descriptive and thematic information in works of art seems to us quite fundamental. It is, of course, true that there are logical constraints affecting the co-occurrence of certain classes of thematic elements with certain classes of descriptive elements in given propositions. In the following section, we shall attempt to identify and to define some traditionally important thematic and descriptive classes and their logical interrelationships.

A,iv. Predicate Types

Themes may be classed either lexically or syntactically. In the present context, we shall be concerned exclusively with syntactic criteria for distinguishing thematic types. We shall attempt to show that, from a critical point of view, the most interesting thematic classes can best be identified on the basis of differences in Predicate structure. Furthermore, it would seem that we need to deal with only four basic Predicate structures in defining the critical notions traditionally considered most useful. These structures may be diagrammed in the following way:

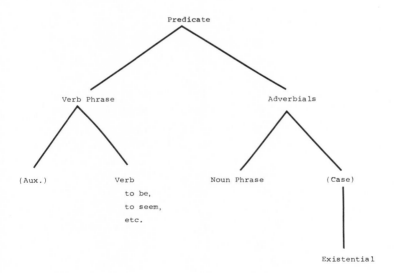

Type 1

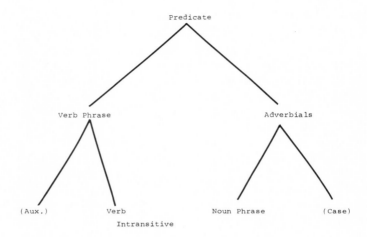

Type 2

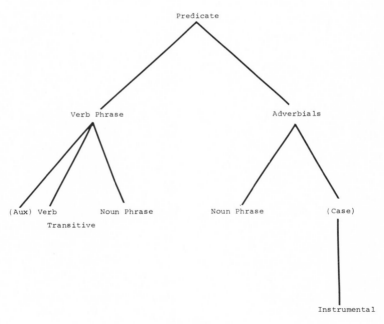

Type 3

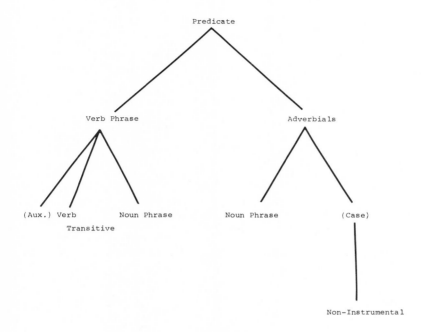

Type 4

Type 1 Predicates involve what may be called "existential" verbs and "existential" adverbials.[6] Since they are true predicates, they belong, however, to assertive rather than to existential propositions.[7] Thus, sentence 1 above, "The house is old," is not a claim that "The old house exists"; rather, it is a report about the state (of being) of "the house." Because sentences containing Type 1 Predicates are, in general, reports about states of being or states of appearance, they are the ones that provide the information concerning the character of individual subjects. Character information, in works of art, has, of course, a peculiarly descriptive flavor. The clearest reason for this connection between character and description would seem to be the absolute necessity for having descriptive, i.e., adverbial, elements in sentences containing Type 1 Predicates. Apparently, the semantic generality of existential verbs requires that they, unlike all other verbs, leave the greater part of the sentence's informational burden to the rest of the predicate. In any case, character information is exclusively concerned with states, specifically states of being. All other information concerning states in works of art is conveyed by sentences containing Type 4 Predicates.

Besides states of being, information about states may include reports of "states of affairs." By a "state of affairs," we mean simply a situation, specifically a static situation involving a relation between one thing and something else. In other words, "states of affairs" are those situations which can be reported by sentences containing transitive verbs that do not take instrumental adverbials.[8] Sentences 7 and 8, for example, are reports of states of affairs. It should be noted that such reports need not contain any descriptive elements. Thus, sentence 7 contains the descriptive expression "passionately," while sentence 8 has no descriptive content. Nonetheless, being reports of states, transitive verbs of the type in question here, like existential verbs, seem more interesting when accompanied by descriptive elements.

Although sentences containing Type 4 Predicates may be more or less interesting depending on their descriptive content, with or without descriptive elements, they are important to the narrative aspect of a work of art. In the most general sense, narration is no more nor less than the recounting of events. Since events inevitably arise from and result in states of affairs, any given narration must include reports of at least two states of affairs, an initial state and a final state. On the other hand, the essence of narration is the reporting of events itself, and we identify the specifically narrative elements in works of art with nonstatic information. Therefore, narrative sentences, i.e., the kind that report events, should all contain Type 2 or Type 3 Predicates.

Narration is primarily concerned with action, and we may say that the Action in a work of art is expressed in narrative propositions, i.e., those that contain intransitive verbs or transitive verbs taking instrumental adverbials. Depending on the kinds of verbs they contain, we may divide narrative sentences fairly neatly into two large groups. First, we shall speak of narrative sentences containing intransitive verbs as those which express the Movement in a work of art. By Movement, we do not mean only those actions which involve motion. On the contrary, Movement can be conceived negatively in terms of such "actions" as eating, sleeping, or even living, where the subject may remain in one place. Sentences 3 and 4 above are reports of Movement.

Second, we shall characterize those narrative sentences containing transitive verbs taking instrumental adverbials as those which convey the Plot in a work of art. Although there may be no explicit precedent for distinguishing Plot from Action in this particular way, we feel that such a distinction brings with it important conceptual and practical advantages. The actions involved in Movement, unlike those involved in Plot, do not comprehend relations between one thing and another. Since both states of affairs and Plot actions do comprehend such relations, they form a natural unit within the work of art. This unit is at the heart of narration; we shall call it the "Story Line." Because states of affairs involve relations between different things, it is obvious that Plot actions which involve other relations between the same things are the essential links in the process of transforming one state into another. Accordingly, Movement actions represent secondary links. They provide practical information and insure verisimilitude.

Finally, it should be clear that the purpose of such an analysis is to identify the specific expressions in a work of art responsible for conveying various aspects of its informational content. Such an identification should permit one to make interesting critical generalizations on the basis of rigorous conceptualizations.

A,v. Noun Phrases and Nouns

There remains one important grammatical category about which we have yet to speak, viz. the category of Noun Phrases and its derivatives. The general structure of the Noun Phrase can be illustrated in the following way:

Noun Phrase→Noun + Determiner

Of course, the Noun is the element of interest here, and we shall discuss Noun Phrases in terms of the Nouns they contain. As we have indicated in previous diagrams, Nouns can occur both in the Subject and in the Predicate of a proposition. However, taken as one (syntactically) undifferentiated group, Nouns share only a certain lexical interest. That is, they, along with Verbs, provide the conceptual elements in propositional information. On the other hand, a classification of Nouns in their specific roles as parts of Subjects, Verb Phrases, and Adverbials yields logical support to certain critical notions. We have already spoken of the descriptive function of Nouns in Adverbials. Thus, we can limit our attention to the Nouns contained in Subjects and Verb Phrases.

It will be remembered that Subject Nouns, as a group, constitute the critical category, Subject Matter, introduced earlier. This category may be divided into subcategories of Subjects with specific critical interest. In accordance with the syntactic approach used throughout this Appendix, we shall attempt to classify Subject Nouns on the basis of their co-occurrence with given Predicate Types. In other words, Subjects co-occurring with Type 4 Predicates, for example, might constitute a class distinct from Subjects co-occurring with Type 1 Predicates. Because Predicate Types determine sentence types, we can say that Subjects may be classified according to the types of sentences in which they occur, e.g., Plot sentences, Character sentences, etc. Of course, the classification of Subject Nouns on the basis of their co-occurrence with certain Predicate Types, i.e., with certain types of Verbs, may seem more semantic than syntactic in nature. However, it must be noted that semantic categories can ultimately be constituted on purely distributional i.e., syntactic, grounds without recourse to notional arguments.

To begin, we may distinguish between sentence types requiring animate subjects and those not requiring such subjects. Grammatically, only Type 1 Predicates can co-occur with nonanimate subjects; Type 2, 3, and 4 Predicates must, on the contrary, be accompanied by animate subjects.[9] It should be immediately clear that nonanimate Nouns can never occur as subjects in sentences involving action or states of affairs. This fact at least partially accounts for the necessity of "human interest" in narration.[10] Conversely, it provides that nonanimate Nouns can only figure as subjects in more or less descriptive sentences. Since any Noun, animate or nonanimate, can be the subject of a Type 1 Predicate sentence and, since such sentences are primarily descriptive (of things), we shall refer to the subjects of such sentences, generally, as the "object-things" of a work of art. Like the class of nonanimate Subject Nouns, the class of animate Subject Nouns seems to have little critical interest in itself. However, this class may be further subdivided.

Perhaps the most important division of the class of animate Subjects, for critical purposes, corresponds to the distinction made earlier between Story Line and Movement sentences. Movement information in works of art contributes mainly to the creation of an impression of verisimilitude. The Story Line, on the other hand, expresses all of the interrelationships among the object-things of a work. Among the morphological critics in the Formalist tradition, such as Propp, Bremond, Souriau, Greimas, and Todorov, the establishment of relational archetypes from Story Line information has always been of paramount importance. Consequently, these critics have been almost exclusively preoccupied with such (primarily) narrative genres as the folktale, drama, and "le récit." We shall attempt to improve on the general form of the "modèles actantiels" developed for various narrative genres by incorporating them into a comprehensive system of morphological analysis.

Undoubtedly, the most complete study of "l'analyse actantielle" to date is that of A. J. Greimas, in his *Sémantique struc-*

turale. We shall take this work as representative of the Formalist tradition and base our remarks on it. Although the Formalists have, in general, limited their attention to fairly restricted corpuses, it can be admitted that their work is aimed at the establishment of at least some of the universals of narrative structure. Greimas, in particular, has attempted to universalize the work of his predecessors in pointing out similarities among their various formulations.

As we have said, "l'analyse actantielle" is concerned with the establishment of relational structures, i.e., with the establishment of (universal) classes of object-things, the archetypal "dramatis personae" of the Story Line. The classes in question correspond to the traditional notions of "Hero," "Villain," etc. Often, the Formalists have sought to characterize genres in terms of their actantial contents and structures. It is the concordance of such formulations as those of Propp and Souriau, for example, that leads Greimas to speak of "le récit," i.e., the narrative in general. Unfortunately, Greimas takes the narrative to be a genre in itself and maintains that "l'analyse actantielle," in fact, is capable of characterizing genres. As we have shown, the narrative element is but a part of the informational content of a work of art and can be characterized quite simply on the basis of sentence form. The generic interest of the "modèles actantiels" is, therefore, secondary. Of course, the actantial classes developed in these models need not be rejected for this reason. On the contrary, since they suggest a basis for defining such traditional critical notions as that of the "hero," they are of particular interest here.

For Greimas, there are six major actantial categories which he calls "Sujet," "Objet," "Destinateur," "Destinataire," "Adjuvant," and "Opposant." It is clear that these categories are not derived from purely syntactic considerations.[11] For example, we might well agree that all of the subjects of sentences containing transitive verbs in a given work can be designated as members of a class, although we find the label "Sujet" unsuitable for a class which does not include all logical subjects. Similarly, we might agree that all Direct Objects can be designated as members of a class, or that all subjects of sentences containing Indirect Objects or that all Indirect Objects can be so designated. In these cases, the class labels are unimportant, for the classes can, in fact, be syntactically defined. However, in the case of the classes labeled "Adjuvant" and "Opposant," there is no major syntactic distinction between "Sujet" and "Adjuvant" or "Sujet" and "Opposant." In all three instances, these actants represent logical subjects of sentences containing transitive verbs. The only distinctions made among these actants are based on the semantic content, i.e., the meaning, of the verbs with which they co-occur. For example, X is an "Opposant" in the sentence: X blocks Y's path. Y is a "Sujet" in the sentence: Y saves the treasure. Z is an "Adjuvant" in the sentence: Z helps Y kill X. In short, although the semantic contents of the predicates of these sentences can ultimately be distinguished on syntactic grounds, their differences have only been perceived notionally by Formalist critics. We postulate that the lack of major syntactic, i.e., distributional, differences among the three actants mentioned reflects a certain genetic unity. This point can best be explained in terms of the nonidentity of actants with actors, i.e. with the individual object-things of a given work.

Greimas has pointed out that one actor, i.e., one "character" in a narrative, can often assume the functions of more than one actant. That is, he may both be "Sujet" and "Destinateur," "Sujet" and "Destinataire," etc. Moreover, more than one actor may assume the functions of a single actant. This point is extremely interesting, since it leads to the abandonment of the traditional, though highly inadequate, identification of archetypal functions with individual actors, or characters. Of course, the most obvious instance of such identification is that of the "protagonist" and the "hero." However, less obvious cases involve greater theoretical inadequacies. Finally, although "l'analyse actantielle" is a step in the right direction, the Formalists have never completely forsaken the character-function idea.

The Formalist distinction among the actantial classes of

"Sujet," "Adjuvant," and "Opposant" is a case in point. As Greimas observes, the "récit" invariably concerns an initial State of Affairs involving a desiring "Destinataire" and a desired "Objet." The desired "Objet" is obtained for the desirer by the "Sujet" (Hero) who is, in general, aided by an "Adjuvant" and hindered by an "Opposant." Since these three categories can be manifested by more than three characters, it is unfair to accuse the Formalists of a theoretical confusion of actants and actors on this level. However, it is interesting to note that the (Plot) actions of these actants, whether positive or negative, all lead to the eventual attainment of the desired "Objet." Whatever the relative importance of the "Sujet," the "Adjuvant," or the "Opposant" may be, in any given narrative, the desired "Objet" is always obtained. By comparison, the possibility of varying the emphasis placed on the activities of any one of the three actants in question indicates that they are not the most fundamental categories of narrative structure. It can even be shown that the categories of "Adjuvant" and "Opposant" are sometimes not manifested at all among the characters of existing narratives. In any case, it seems to us theoretically necessary to account for the variable importance of certain actants. This problem is but part of a larger question involving the possibilities for manifesting, in a cast of characters, the basic structure of the narrative.

We take the position that narrative structure can best be described by a set of rules similar to those of a generative grammar. With such a set of rules, rules which would generate Plot structures in particular, constants and variables can be systematically indicated. For example, a generative grammar of Plot structure should be able to illustrate the fact that all of the characters derived from the categories of "Sujet," "Adjuvant," and "Opposant" are also derived from one, fundamental category of (logical) Subjects. Since the actions of any logical Subject in a work can belong to the Plot which leads to a final State of Affairs involving the gratification of an initial desire, it is reasonable to identify the "Accomplishing Subject" function with the "Heroic" function. In this sense, the "Sujet," the "Adjuvant," and even the "Opposant" functions represent aspects of the "Heroic."

It should be noted here that a generative grammar of Plot structure need not be limited to the determination of degrees of constancy or variability among major and minor categories. On the contrary, the output of such a grammar should, in principle, include the full range of possible Plot sentences. Because these sentences contain lexical elements, the grammar of Plot structure must contain lexical rules and must be accompanied by a lexicon of actors and actions. Finally, it is on the basis of their lexical contents that works containing Story Lines can be classified into (narrative) genres.

We have argued that genres can be identified notionally in terms of the specific feelings of pleasure derived from appreciations of generically similar works. These feelings of pleasure co-occur with the repression of desires, which, in at least some cases, are related to or identical with the desires gratified in the Story Lines of so-called narratives. Since the lexical elements in Story Line information provide the clues to the specific desires and gratifications involved in the narrative parts of given works, their presence in different combinations can be used as a criterion for genre identification. By matching specific aesthetic effects to specific Plot sentence distributions and their derivations, therefore, the subjective characterization of certain genres can be supported and, to some extent, replaced by a formal, structural one. In Chapter 3 of this work, we present a generative model for the derivation of Tragic Plots.

Notes

1. Tragic Thought

1. The periods during which tragic thought flourished in Greece, Rome, England, and France, for example, are all characterized by the appearance of a great "monarch-hero"—Pericles, Augustus, Elizabeth I, Louis XIV—whose reign followed closely on some great popular disaster or upheaval—the plague in Athens, the transformation of the republic into an empire, religious and civil wars, etc.

2. See Chapter 3.

3. For a discussion of the particular sense of the term "mimesis" used in this work, see section 2, iii.

4. It is interesting to note that the peculiarly Christian tragic in art, which can be specifically associated with extreme Calvinism, can do completely without traditional heroes. This fact is illustrated in the works of certain poets of the Reformation, such as Garnier and D'Aubigné. All that is necessary in these works is the portrayal of great suffering. Although the tableaux of suffering in Dante, for example, are, perhaps, equal in violence to those in D'Aubigné, the earlier writer never quite abandons the Classical model and always features some sort of hero, be it Ugolino or Judas.

5. A. C. Bradley, *Shakespearean Tragedy* (New York: St. Martin's Press, 1966), p. 29.

2. Belief and Information

1. Our usage of the term "belief-reaction" here may evoke associations with the Bloomfieldian usage of the term "meaning." We do not, however, wish to imply that the "meaning" of an utterance is, in any way, identical to the "belief-reaction" appropriate to its perception. Furthermore, it must be emphasized that "belief-reactions" are not to be thought of in purely behavioral terms. They may be conceived behaviorally, as acts, and psychologically, as feelings, as sensations and, of course, as beliefs.

2. For a discussion of the notion of "kernel sentences", see Noam

Chomsky, *Aspects of the Theory of Syntax* (Cambridge: MIT Press, 1965).

3. For a discussion of the notion of utterance-derivation in grammatical theory, see Ibid.

4. For a general discussion of the psychoanalytic position concerning artistic pleasure-production, see Sarah Kofman, *L'enfance de l'art* (Paris: Payot, 1970).

5. For a discussion of these psychological mechanisms, see Ernest Jones, *Papers on Psycho-Analysis* (Boston: Beacon Press, 1957).

6. For an amplified discussion of these remarks, see Bradley Berke, "A Generative View of Mimesis" in *Poetics,* Spring 1978.

7. For a discussion of the terms *"signifiant"* and *"signifié"* as they are used here, see Ferdinand de Saussure, *Cours de Linguistique générale* (Paris: Payot, 1969).

8. The notions of "actor" and "actant" are explained in the Appendix. For a detailed discussion, see A. J. Greimas, *Sémantique structurale* (Paris: Larousse, 1966).

3. A Grammar of Tragic Myth

1. Throughout this study, we shall be using the term "Plot" in a very particular way. For a discussion of the technical sense of the term "Plot" and the relation of Plot to other aspects of information contained in works of art, see the Appendix.

2. The case of *Phèdre* will be discussed in detail in Chapter 5. We shall maintain that the tragic nature of this play depends to a great extent on the circumstances of its presentation.

3. See previous discussion of derivation in Chapter 2.

4. For a discussion of the various aspects of personality structure, see Sigmund Freud, *The Ego and the Id* (London: The Hogarth Press, 1968).

5. The symbol " . . . " in this rule indicates an indeterminately long string of identical symbols "M_1'", "M_2'" or "F'", as the case may be.

6. This hypothesis remains to be proven. At present, too little evidence is available regarding female psychosexuality to take any definitive position.

7. The case of *Romeo and Juliet* is discussed below in detail. Here, we are referring to the love-tragedy, as opposed to the political tragedy, of *Romeo and Juliet.*

8. Here, we are referring to the secondary Tragic Plot of the play, the one involving Hamlet, Polonius, Laertes, and Ophelia.

9. Here, we are referring to the "main" Tragic Plot of *Hamlet,* the one concerning Hamlet, Claudius, Gertrude, and the old king.

10. Here, we are referring to the "political" Tragic Plot of *Romeo and Juliet.* This Tragic Plot is discussed below in detail.

11. For a discussion of the concept of *le nom du Père* as a theoreti-

cally more adequate notion than that of the father as a legal authority, see Jacques Lacan, *Ecrits* (Paris: Editions du Seuil, 1966).

12. Among the recent attempts adequately to reformulate Freudian Oedipal theory, those of René Girard deserve some mention here. In his *Violence and the Sacred,* for example, Girard relates the specific conflicts of the Oedipus complex to more general, binary relations such as rivalry. Although far from the philosophical fancifulness and sometimes silly biologism of Deleuze and Guattari in their *Anti-Oedipe,* Girard's work is content to fit the Oedipal situation into a finite set of isotopic phenomena. Our position is radically different from this interesting approach whose fertility is, however, limited by the pragmatic constraints of cultural anthropology. Our model is based on a logical functionalism that is anthropological, but only to the extent that it depends on the categories of natural language.

13. For a psychoanalytic discussion of this point with relation to tragedy, see E. Sharpe, "L'impatience d'Hamlet," reprinted in *Hamlet et Oedipe,* Ernest Jones (Paris: Gallimard, 1967).

14. The symbol ISA is always rewritten as a positive entity for the sake of economy and simplicity. All voiding of unessential Plot sentences can be accomplished on the level of Rules 6, 10, 11, and 12.

15. A minor selectional rule will provide that the only act an M_2 can commit with regard to an M_1 is that of banishment. No really violent act can be imagined here. Moreover, an M_2 can only commit a destructive act of banishment on an M_1 when an M_2' commits a more violent destructive act on that M_1. Examples are extremely rare, but the phenomena can be seen in *Romeo and Juliet* and in *Hippolytus.*

4. The Central Desire Triangle of Tragic Myth

1. A. C. Bradley maintains that every genuine Shakespearean tragedy ends with the death of the hero. Because this factor is obviously unessential in tragedy in general, Bradley's position may be seen as begging the question of *Troilus and Cressida.*

2. In *The Merchant of Venice,* homosexual elements include the transvestitism of Portia and her servant and the exchange of love tokens with the lovers disguised as men. If any tragedies featuring homosexual Central Desire Triangles exist, their obscurity is probably due to the inability of the average spectator to relate tragically to homosexual desires.

3. It might be suggested here, though in a very tentative way, that the "para-tragicness" of possible dramatic situations can be measured in terms of the lateness of voiding of these situations in Plot generations using the specific psychological performance model for tragedy.

5. Tragic and Nontragic Variants

˚1. This possibility is not to be ignored. In fact, the amount of attention the spectator pays to the text of a play may vary greatly with external circumstances. If the spectator feels he knows the "story," for example, he may pay much more attention to the lexical and optical aspects of the presentation of a play than to the informational aspects of the work.

2. For a technical definition of the term "state of affairs," as it is used here, see the Appendix.

Appendix

1. For a discussion of intersemiotic translation and the possibility of expressing the same semantic content in various semiotic codes, see Roman Jakobson, *Essais de Linguistique Générale* (Paris: Les Editions de Minuit, 1963), Chapter 4.

2. Various criteria for the standardization of information in works of art have been suggested by critics using so-called morphological approaches. For what is perhaps the most adequate and useful discussion, see A. J. Greimas, *Sémantique structurale* (Paris: Larousse, 1966).

3. For an explanation of the notion of "kernel sentences," see Noam Chomsky, 1965a.

4. For a discussion of the notions of "phrase structure" and the "base component" of grammatical descriptions, see Ibid.

5. See Charles Hockett, *A Course in Modern Linguistics* (New York: MacMillan, 1958).

6. The so-called Predicate Adjectives that accompany verbs like "to be" or "to seem" are adverbials in the sense that they describe states and not subjects, when they are used in genuine predicates, i.e., in genuine assertions. The verbs in question here are being used to report states and not as simple logical copulae.

7. For a discussion of the distinction between existential and assertive propositions, see, for example, P. F. Strawson, *Individuals* (London: Methuen, 1959).

8. Transitive verbs that take instrumental adverbs are, invariably, the kinds of verbs that one uses to report events. They signify actions, movement, etc. Thus, they are not suited to the reporting of states.

9. The notion of animacy used here is a grammatical one. The class of animate Nouns corresponds distributionally to the class of transitive verbs, because sentences containing these verbs can undergo passive transformations. That is, the subjects of these sentences must, in some sense, be agents in relation to other things which represent patients.

10. The criterion of human interest in narration has been discussed by numerous critics. Among the Formalists who have been concerned with this problem, see A. J. Greimas, *Sémantique structurale* (Paris: Larousse, 1966), and T. Todorov, *Grammaire du Décaméron* (The Hague: Mouton, 1969).
11. Greimas insists on this point himself. See Greimas, 1966.

Bibliography

Abel, Lionel. *Moderns on Tragedy.* Greenwich, Conn.: Pawcott, 1967.

Aeschylus. *The Complete Greek Tragedies.* Vols. 1 & 2. D. Greene and R. Latimore (eds.). Chicago: University of Chicago Press, 1959.

Aristotle. *Poetics,* trans. Bywater, I., in McKeon, R. (ed.) *Basic Works of Aristotle.* New York: Random House, 1968.

Auerbach, E. *Mimesis.* Princeton: Princeton University Press, 1953.

Austin, J. L. *How to Do Things with Words.* Cambridge: Harvard University Press, 1962.

Bach, Emon. *An Introduction to Transformational Grammars.* New York: Holt, Rinehart, and Winston, 1964.

——— "Subcategories in Transformational Grammar," *Proceedings of the Ninth International Congress of Linguists.* The Hague: Mouton, 1964.

Bar-Hillel, Y. *Language and Information.* Reading, MA: Addison-Wesley, 1964.

Bloomfield, Leonard. *Language.* New York: Holt, 1933.

Bloomfield, M. "A Grammatical Approach to Personification Allegory," Modern Philology, 60, 1963, pp. 161–171.

Bowra, Sir Maurice. *Sophoclean Tragedy.* Oxford: Clarendon Press, 1944.

Bradley, A. C. *Shakespearean Tragedy.* New York: St. Martin's Press, 1966.

Carnap, Rudolf. *Meaning and Necessity.* Chicago: University of Chicago Press, 1956.

Carroll, I. *Language and Thought.* Englewood Cliffs: Prentice-Hall, 1964.

Chomsky, Noam. *Syntactic Structures.* The Hague: Mouton, 1957.

——— "A Transformational Approach to Syntax," in Fodor and Katz (eds.) *The Structure of Language.* Englewood Cliffs: Prentice-Hall, 1964.

——— *Aspects of the Theory of Syntax.* Cambridge: MIT Press, 1965a.

——— "Three Models for the Description of Language," in Luce, Bush, and Galanter (eds.) *Readings in Mathematical Psychology,* Vol. II. New York: Wiley, 1965b.

Communications: 8. Paris: Editions du Seuil, 1966.

Deleuze, G. and Guattari, F. *L'Anti-Oedipe,* Editions de Minuit, Paris, 1972.

Ebeling, C. L. *Linguistic Units.* The Hague: Mouton, 1960.

Else, Gerard. *Aristotle's Poetics: the Argument.* Cambridge: Harvard University Press, 1957.

———— *The Origin and Early Form of Greek Tragedy.* Cambridge: Harvard University Press, 1965.

———— "Imitation in the Fifth Century," *Classical Philology,* LIII, 1958, pp. 73–90.

Euripides. *The Complete Greek Tragedies,* Vols. 5, 6. D. Greene and R. Latimore (eds.). Chicago: University of Chicago Press, 1959.

———— Hippolytus, ed. W.S. Barrett. Oxford: Clarendon Press, 1963.

Foucault, Michel. "Nietszche, Freud, et Marx," *Nietzsche,* Cahiers de Royaumont VI. Paris: Editions de Minuit, 1967.

Freud, Sigmund. *Complete Works.* 24 vols. ed. James Strachey. London: The Hogarth Press, 1968.

———— 1900. *The Interpretation of Dreams.* Vols. IV and V.

———— 1905. *Three Essays on the Theory of Sexuality,* Vol. VII.

———— 1906. *Psychopathic Characters on the Stage,* Vol. VII.

———— 1907. *Jensen's "Gradiva,"* Vol. IX.

———— 1908. *Creative Writers and Day-Dreaming,* Vol. IX.

———— 1910. *Leonardo da Vinci and a Memory of His Childhood,* Vol. XI.

———— 1910. *The Antithetical Meaning of Primal Words,* Vol. XI.

———— 1910. *A Special Type of Choice of Object Made by Men,* Vol. XI.

———— 1910. *Contributions to a Discussion on Suicide,* Vol. XI.

———— 1913. *Totem and Taboo,* Vol. XIII.

———— 1913. *The Claims of Psycho-Analysis to Scientific Interest,* Vol. XIII.

———— 1914. *The Moses of Michelangelo,* Vol. XIII.

———— 1920. *Beyond the Pleasure Principle,* Vol. XVIII.

———— 1923. *The Ego and the Id,* Vol. XIX.

———— 1923. *Remarks on the Theory and Practice of Dream-Interpretation,* Vol. XVIII.

———— 1928. *Dostoevsky and Parricide,* Vol. XXI.

———— 1930. *Civilization and its Discontents,* Vol. XXI.

———— 1939. *Moses and Monotheism,* Vol. XXIII.

———— 1940. *The Splitting of the Ego in the Process of Defense,* Vol. XXIII.

Girard, R. *Violence and the Sacred.* Baltimore: Johns Hopkins Press, 1977.

Green, A. *Un Oeil en Trop.* Paris: Editions de Minuit, 1969.

Greenburg, J. *Universals in Language.* Cambridge: MIT Press, 1963.

Greimas, A. J. *Sémantique structurale.* Paris: Larousse, 1966.

Harris, Zellig. *Methods in Structural Linguistics.* Chicago: University of Chicago Press, 1951.

Hegel. G. W. F. *Samtliche Werke.* 20 vols. ed. Hermann Glockner. Stuttgart: Frommann, 1927–30.
———— *The Phenomenology of Mind.* trans. J. Baille. London: Allen and Unwin, Ltd., 1966.
Heidegger, Martin. *Being and Time.* trans. J. Macquarrie and E. Robinson. New York: Harper, 1962.
Hjelmslev, Louis. *Prolegomena to a Theory of Language,* trans. F. Whitfield. Bloomington: Indiana University Press, 1953.
Hockett, Charles. *A Course in Modern Linguistics.* New York: MacMillan, 1958.
Homer. *The Iliad of Homer,* trans. R. Lattimore. Chicago: University of Chicago Press, 1951.
———— *The Odyssey of Homer,* trans. R. Lattimore. New York: Harper, 1967.

Jaeger, W. *Peideia: The Ideals of Greek Culture.* 3 vols. trans. G. Highet. New York: Oxford University Press, 1945.
Jakobson, Roman. *Essais de Linguistique générale.* Paris: Les Editions de Minuit, 1963.
James, William. *A Pluralistic Universe.* New York: Longmans, Green, 1909.
Jones, Ernest. *Hamlet et Oedipe,* trans. Anne-Marie Le Gall. Paris: Gallimard, 1967.
———— *Papers on Psycho-Analysis.* Boston: Beacon Press, 1967.

Kaufmann, Walter. *From Shakespeare to Existentialism.* Boston: Beacon Press, 1959.
Kirk, G.S. and J.E. Raven. *The Presocratic Philosophers.* Cambridge: Cambridge University Press, 1954.
Kitto, H.O.F. *Sophocles: Dramatist and Philosopher.* London: Oxford University Press, 1958.
Klima, E. E. "Negation in English," in Fodor and Katz (eds.). *The Structure of Language.* Englewood Cliffs: Prentice-Hall, 1964.
Kofman, Sarah. *L'Enfance de l'Art.* Paris: Payot, 1970.
Koutsoudas, A. *Writing Transformational Grammars.* New York: McGraw-Hill, 1967.

Lacan, Jacques. *Ecrits.* Paris: Editions du Seuil, 1966.
La Chastelaine de Vergi. ed. G. Raynaud. Paris: Champion, 1972.
Lattimore, Richmond. *Story Patterns in Greek Tragedy.* Ann Arbor: University of Michigan Press, 1964.
Lees, R. *The Grammar of English Nominalizations.* The Hague: Mouton, 1960.
Lessing, G. E. *Laokoon.* Berlin: Voss, 1766.

Morris, Charles, W. *Signs, Language and Behavior.* Englewood Cliffs: Prentice-Hall, 1955.

Nietzsche, Frederich. *The Birth of Tragedy,* trans. W. Kaufmann. New York: Vintage Books, 1966.

———— *Beyond Good and Evil,* trans. W. Kaufmann. New York: Vintage Books, 1966.

———— *On the Genealogy of Morals,* trans. W. Kaufmann. New York: Vintage Books, 1966.

———— *The Case of Wagner,* trans. W. Kaufmann. New York: Vintage Books, 1966.

———— *Ecce Homo,* trans. W. Kaufmann. New York: Vintage Books, 1966.

———— *Basic Writings of Nietzsche,* trans. W. Kaufmann. New York: Random House, 1968.

———— *The Antichrist,* trans. W. Kaufmann in *The Portable Nietzsche.* New York: Vintage Books, 1954.

———— *Thus Spake Zarathustra,* trans. W. Kaufmann in *The Portable Nietzsche.* New York: Viking Press, 1954.

———— *Twilight of the Idols,* trans. W. Kaufmann in *The Portable Nietzsche.* New York: Viking Press, 1954.

Plato. *The Dialogues of Plato.* 2 vols. trans. B. Jowett. New York: Random House, 1938.

Postal, Paul. *Constituent Structure: A Study of Contemporary Models of Syntactic Description.* The Hague: Mouton, 1964.

Racine, Jean. *Oeuvres Complètes.* Paris: Garnier, 1961.

Rank, Otto. *The Myth of the Birth of the Hero.* New York: Vintage Books, 1964.

Rosenberg, J. and Charles Travis. *Readings in the Philosophy of Language.* Englewood Cliffs: Prentice-Hall, 1971.

Russell, Bertrand. *An Inquiry into Meaning and Truth.* Baltimore: Pelican Books, 1962.

Ryle, Gilbert. *The Concept of Mind.* London: Penguin Books, 1963.

Sartre, Jean-Paul. *La Nausée.* Paris: Gallimard, 1938.

———— *L'Etre et le Néant.* Paris: Gallimard, 1943.

———— *Les Mouches.* Paris: Gallimard, 1943.

———— *L'Existentialisme est un humanisme.* Paris: Nagel, 1946.

Saussure, Ferdinand de. *Cours de Linguistique générale.* Paris: Payot, 1969.

Schopenhauer, Arthur. *The World as Will and Representation.* New York: Dover Books, 1969.

Shakespeare, William. *The Complete Works.* ed. George Lyman Kittredge. Boston: Cinn, 1936.

Sharpe, E. "L'impatience d'Hamlet," trans. Anne-Marie Le Gall in Ernest Jones, *Hamlet et Oedipe.* Paris: Gallimard, 1967.

Skinner, B. F. *Verbal Behavior.* New York: Appleton, Century and Crofts, 1957.

Sophocles. *The Complete Greek Tragedies.* Vols. 3 & 4. D. Greene and R. Lattimore (eds.). Chicago: University of Chicago Press, 1959.

Spinoza. *Ethics.* New York: Dover Books.

Starobinski, Jean. "Hamlet et Freud," *Les Temps Modernes,* April, 1967.

Strawson, P.F. *Individuals.* London: Methuen, 1959.

———— "On Referring," in Rosenberg, J. and Charles Travis (eds.) *Readings in the Philosophy of Language.* Englewood Cliffs: Prentice-Hall, 1971.

Todorov, Tzvetan. *Grammaire du Décaméron.* The Hague: Mouton, 1969.

Vernant, J.P. *Mythe et Pensée chez les Grecs.* Paris: Maspéro, 1965.

Wittgenstein, L. *Philosophical Investigations,* trans. G. E. M. Anscombe. New York: MacMillan, 1953.